# FLESH

BY RICK JAMES

"FLESH"
Written by Rick James
Edit by Christina Marty

Book and cover design by Aaron Martin
www.iamaaronmartin.com

Cru Publishing
100 Lake Hart Drive, 2500
Orlando, FL 32832-0100

To order go to CruPress.com

International Standard Book Number: 1-56399-229-9

# TABLE OF CONTENTS

## PREFACE TO THE REVISED FLESH

I wrote Flesh about a dozen years ago, and while many books need a refresh at some point, anything written on lust and pornography before the advent of the iPhone is about as relevant as the Amish. That's a bit of an overstatement because sin is still sin and lust is still lust, but this refresh is more of a rewrite, requiring far more than a change in copyright to bring it current. And that's what I've done. Same biblical teaching but applied to a context different from the world that existed in 2003.

In this writing of Flesh you'll find most of the articles updated in one way or another, as well as the addition of five or six new articles. The devotionals have also been rewritten, though I stayed with most of the same passages. The only thing that didn't change is the Bible studies because there we are dealing with timeless truth that speaks to all humans, everywhere, at all times. I probably could have updated a few of the questions though, but felt my efforts being hindered by laziness and a pervasive sense of "good enough." Just being honest. That also hasn't changed from the original.

Oh, and just so we're clear: this book won't fix you. It will help you understand the problems and issues better; it will help you understand sanctification better; it will encourage you in your struggle; it will help you to persevere in your struggle; it will shed light on certain passages and teachings of Scripture; it will help you to metabolize the grace and forgiveness that is ours in Christ; but it will not fix you. God will fix us all someday, but in the meantime all we can do is grow and this book will help you in your growth, as you "grow with a growth that is from God" (Colossians 2:19).

Rick James

# INTRODUCTION

My wife and I live in creaky 1950's Cape Cod style house. Our house is an open door to all of God's creatures, but not in a good way. Stink bugs, mice, spiders: everybody finds their way in. Last year about this time we were dealing with a squirrel problem. I could literally hear the critters moving nuts around inside the walls. So how exactly do you get rid of squirrels once they've moved in?

I didn't know, but from nibbled food on the kitchen counter, I could tell that the first step was to clean the counter and keep it clean. A few days later I found evidence of the squirrels in the cabinets under the counter. So we cleaned out the cabinets. Then I found a bag of food in the pantry that had clearly been gnawed by some critter, so the pantry got cleaned and organized (while we were at it), but still the squirrels. Soon, I imagined, would come the circulars and bills in the mail addressed to Bob and Carol Squirrel.

So the vermin hunt took me outside the house so I could determine where to find the critters' entrance. Two locations seemed promising: a rotting piece of fascia board and a bent gutter. I fixed them both, if you consider smashing something with a hammer fixing it. I think all this really accomplished was sealing them inside the house because a few days later I heard their patter coming from the ceiling. So the attic got an inspection as did the cellar.

I know you're on the edge of your seat, so I'll cut to the chase. The 'squirrels' had nested behind the dishwasher, and they weren't squirrels, they were mice. True story. The story isn't very interesting *or* hard to believe, so I can't imagine why it wouldn't be true. Kind of like saying, "I went to the bank — true story."

## FLESH

The mice, aka squirrels, in this story are a metaphor for lust and pornography, but I imagine you already knew that. The story isn't really about them; it is about my quest to get rid of them, how motivated I was and how, in the process, the entire home got cleaned and put in order. The perspective and path taken is laid out in these articles. Let me spell it out a little clearer.

However porn or lust or homosexuality or fetishism or sexting or whatever got into your life, it has gotten in if you're reading this book. As God's children, we don't want this kind of junk in our lives, so we're fairly motivated to get rid of it.

There are few leverage-able areas in our lives where we are miserable or motivated enough that we'd do anything to come to resolution. Finding a mate is one — we'd do just about anything to get that squared away. Squirrels moving in...that's another one. And then there are certain sins that sort of own us and we'd do just about anything to be free from them. Freedom and enslavement are highly motivating, and God leverages these for our greatest good. When I say "leverage," I mean he uses a particular issue to get to a whole bunch of others because we're consigned to doing anything to be rid of whatever it is. We're a captive audience (we're not going anywhere until it's fixed) and we are motivated pupils. Think of God's interaction with Israel. They had a million problems and almost all of them got addressed by parking an enemy army on their border. A captive audience equals a motivated pupil.

Cleaning and straightening the house is also a good picture of the inter-relatedness of spiritual issues in our lives — positive and negative. For example, a lack of Christian community, prayerlessness, too much time alone, struggles with anxiety and depression, a schedule that flips days and nights, all of these factors contribute to a struggle with pornography, and therefore, growth in purity will have ties to growth in other areas. We are whole, integrated people and there's just no way around that.

It seems that there's a pill for everything. I bet if I went to my doctor and told him that whenever I eat Mexican food my toes swell to the size of a baseball gloves, he'd have a pill for it. Somewhere someone makes a pill for swelling toes caused by Mexican food. I bet it's bright and purple and mediciney and has a name that sounds like zenocab.

It would be great if we could take a pill for lust, a capsule just before bed, like Lunesta. Obviously we can't. What is not so obvious is this mindset of looking to a single, isolated solution. People seem supremely confident that if you just "do" this, or "realize" that, or "understand" who you are, or who God is, the problem will evaporate. And if that one thing, whatever it is, doesn't work, then the ultimate solution is clear: "Go see a counselor." We treat counselors like Lunesta too.

The following articles are written from a certain perspective about the way God works, a very biblical perspective. This is an approach that is cooperative with God (involving our participation), comprehensive (touching on many related issues), biblical (focused on sanctification and spiritual growth), and in concert with community and mission (other-centered, outward focused).

Each article in the series will deal with a different subject and each subject contributes in some way toward our growth in purity. I hope you find in them encouragement, wisdom, strength, and endurance for the battle against Flesh.

Rick James

# BY DESIGN

---

## IMPLICATIONS OF GENDER AND MARRIAGE
## BEING CREATED BY GOD

There is no original evil. As Peter Kreeft writes: "Evil can't be greater than good, because evil is a bent good, a diseased good, a parasite on good." You cannot have destruction without something to destroy. You cannot have bulimia without the joy of eating to corrupt. You cannot have sexual immorality, perversion, and pornography if the beauty and joy of sex and marriage had not come first. So, before we discuss lust, sexual immorality, pornography, and the like, we need to begin here, with God's original design. We need to begin with the beauty of marriage and the goodness of sex, back when God called everything "good."

> Then God said, "Let us make man in our image, in our likeness, and let them rule over the fish of the sea and the birds of the air, over the livestock, over all the earth, and over all the creatures that move along the ground." So God created man in his own image, in the image of God he created him; male and female he created them."
> Genesis 1:26, 27

### Marriage and Sex: A Picture of God in Three Persons

When you read Genesis 1:26 and 27, what stands out is the peculiar *plurality* of the *singular* creation called "man." The passage says that God "created man" (singular) and man (singular) was created "male and female" (plural). It's sort of odd and sort of awesome that man and woman *together* are the image of God. Being made in God's image no doubt has other design implications (like our capacity to rule over the planet), but it is clearly a reflection of God's relational nature: one God in three persons (God the Father, God the Son, God the Holy Spirit).

Twentieth century theologian Karl Barth put it this way: "Man never exists as such, but always as the human male or female ... Nor can he wish to liberate himself from the relationship and be man without woman or woman apart from man."

Think, then, of the profundity of sex within the context of marriage as two, literally, become one flesh. Is there anything else on this blue–green planet that so reflects the image of one God in three persons? I think not. The greatest miracle of sex is not what it feels like, but what it looks like — what it mirrors about the nature of God. And this is the particular delight of Satan in perverting sexual intimacy and marital oneness: defacing God's image, spray painting it with obscenity. I mean, if you really stop and think about the essence of sexual immorality and how it reflects upon God, it's enough to make you cry, it really is.

Sex not only reflects the unity of God in this structural sort of way (two individuals, one flesh), but it mirrors the reciprocating joy, delight, and supreme satisfaction that overflows between Father, Son, and Holy Spirit. In other words, God is glorified in the *joy* of sex. Sex is fun, fulfilling, and freeing because God designed it to be, not because there is something inherent in the physical sensations that give rise to these feelings.

And finally we might note that sex and marriage were also designed with a view toward re-creating. Love and unity is a creative force that manifests in all manner of growth, fruitfulness, and life with the most obvious example being the fruit of childbearing. All of this is in the design and God's intent for love, sex, and marriage.

### Marriage and Sex: A Picture of God's Relationship with His People

Marriage is not only a reflection of God's relationship within himself, but his relationship with us. In their book, *Authentic Human Sexuality*, Dr. Judith and Jack Balswick define four components of God's marriage design. When lived out, it becomes clear how these elements reflect God's relationship with us. This is the blueprint for marriage.

### 1. Covenantal Commitment

The marriage relationship, like God's relationship with us, was meant to be based on an unconditional covenant commitment. It is a commitment to pursue the other partner regardless of his or her response, for that is what God does with us. The only grounds for breaking covenant love is if the other person leaves and establishes a covenant with another person. Otherwise, each person in the relationship must be unconditionally pursued, much like God pursues us. This should explain why the only ground for divorce given by Jesus is marital unfaithfulness — or, when one partner breaks the covenant the only way possible, by establishing a new one with someone else.

### 2. Grace

The second design principle follows from the first: offering grace, rather than judgment or blame, is what provides healing and renewal within the marriage relationship. How many times does God forgive us when we ask? Always, his grace is bottomless and that is the design for marriage. Marriage ceases to reflect God's relationship with us, and therefore its intended design when one or both partners reach a threshold in their grace giving ("I can forgive this, but not this"). They move from a disposition of grace to an adversarial, judgmental disposition. They look to blame, convict, find fault, or pay back wrongs, rather than forgive. There is nothing quite like hell-on-earth except a graceless adversarial marriage, which is why many end in divorce.

### 3. Empowerment

The third principle of God's design for marriage is that personal gifts and resources are used to affirm the other rather than control. Covenant is the vow to love. Grace is the ability to forgive. Empowerment is the use of power to affirm and strengthen the other. God uses his power to empower us, not to control or manipulate, and this is what marriage is intended to mirror. Marriage is about living to help your partner succeed and doing all within your power to bring this about. I'm sure you have seen marriages in which the ruling dynamic is each partner trying to get his or her own way, each vying for power. This is the relational dynamic of Wall Street, not marriage.

### Knowing and Being Known

Last, marriage was designed to deepen one's experience of knowing and being known. This is the essence of our walk with God, and therefore, this is the essence of the marriage relationship.

For some reason, if you go to Roy Rogers at 7:00 a.m. you will find dozens of old people — really old people — having coffee. As you watch the couples, they seem to have an endless capacity to stare and not communicate with each other. Unfortunately, even with the aid of caffeine, their camaraderie does not increase, and if you speak with them, both answer at the same time, not listening to the other. This is bad advertisement for marriage as well as for Roy Rogers (*Come to Roy Rogers, where you're always alone*). At some point, each partner's knowledge of the other stagnated. Each individual ceased the pursuit of knowing his or her partner. Such relationships, which should grow in intimacy and not boredom, no longer mirror the vitality of God with his people.

This is the blueprint of marriage. Because we have never seen a marriage unmarred by sin, we have never seen its completed construction, but we've seen and experienced glimpses. Because this design was meant to show forth the elements of God's love for us, Satan is always looking to deface the image of marriage and sex. When there is conditional love, divorce, selfishness, isolation, judgment and pettiness, we can no longer see our Father's reflection.

That picture of God's original design for sex and marriage, and the way it was meant to glorify God and speak of his beauty, love, intimacy, unity and grace, should help explain why God has put very specific parameters around how sex and marriage are supposed to function. There is a blueprint to be followed and if one deviates, he or she constructs something that does not mirror the image of God, or worse, creates an image that mocks him.

That is exactly what lust, sexual immorality and pornography do. As God's design for sex and marriage shout to the universe, "Look how great God is!," sexual immorality and pornography scream of self-centeredness, abusive and manipulative love, degradation, and of a God who does not adequately provide, and whose ways are wholly unsatisfying.

This is what is at stake. This is what that battle of purity is really about: we will either be vehicles and vessels that bring praise and glory to God, or pawns used as insults for Satan to hurl against God.

# WORLDS APART

**The difference between being forgiven and feeling forgiven**

In the book, *The Emperor of Scent*, Guy Roberts explains how he came to create Chanel 22, Christian Dior's most famous and profitable perfume. Roberts received a call that a large quantity of ambergris — the critical ingredient of many perfumes — had just been spotted washed up on shore. Ambergris is the lyrical name for what is essentially whale vomit. A whale coughs the stuff up like a cat with a hairball. It then floats on the surface of the ocean for about a decade, decomposes, and the next thing you know, it's worth about $100,000 a yard.

So Roberts shows up, fingers the ambergris to inspect its purity, and because no one wants whale vomit on their hands, he goes to the bathroom and uses the ten cent bar of bathroom soap to clean it off. Several hours later he smells his hands, and that's where got Chanel 22. Something magical happens when vomit and soap come together, and of course I'm talking about forgiveness: the meeting of our moral waste and God's mercy, and they met at the crucifixion of our Lord and Savior, Jesus Christ.

Because Jesus died for our sins, we have been forgiven. Past tense. All of our sin — past, present, and future — has been forgiven — past tense. But as I'm sure you've noticed, being forgiven and *feeling* forgiven are two very different things.

This issue, this problem of *feeling* and *experiencing* forgiveness, is the focal point of the epilogue in John's gospel. Epilogues are about new beginnings, and John's epilogue is about the beginning of the church and a new beginning for Peter, and the two are by no means unrelated. On the night of Jesus' arrest, Peter denies even knowing him, and the days that follow are spent in the haze of guilt and regret. Seeing Jesus on the beach of Galilee, Peter's joy vanquishes his shame, and he runs to meet him. This "meeting on the beach" is orchestrated by Jesus for the purpose of helping his dear friend and disciple to feel forgiven; and I think it would be a good passage to read:

> When they had finished eating, Jesus said to Simon Peter, "Simon son of John, do you truly love me more than these?" "Yes, Lord," he said, "You know that I love you." Jesus said, "Feed my lambs."
>
> Again Jesus said, "Simon, son of John, do you truly love me?" He answered, "Yes, Lord, you know that I love you." Jesus said, "Take care of my sheep."
>
> The third time he said to him, "Simon son of John, do you love me?" Peter was hurt because Jesus asked him the third time, "Do you love me?" He said, "Lord, you know all things; you know that I love you." Jesus said, "Feed my sheep.
>
> "I tell you the truth, when you were younger you dressed yourself and went where you wanted; but when you are old you will stretch out your hands, and someone else will dress you and lead you where you do not want to go." Jesus said this to indicate the kind of death by which Peter would glorify God.
>
> Then he said to him, "Follow me!" Peter turned and saw that the disciple whom Jesus loved was following them. (This was the one who had leaned back against Jesus at the supper and had said, "Lord, who is going to betray you?") When Peter saw him, he asked, "Lord, what about him?"
>
> Jesus answered, "If I want him to remain alive until I return, what is that to you? You must follow me."
> John 21:15-24

Everything that's said in this exchange is expressly for Peter:

for his restoration, and of course for ours. In John's epilogue, something new is going to happen in the history of redemption. For the first time in history, God's people are going to look back instead of forward for the sacrifice for sin. It's really odd that the sins we commit today were forgiven yesterday, but God's plans and purposes have to fit onto a one-dimensional timeline, moving forward like train tracks in a straight line. We're blessed to be on this side of the Cross, but challenged in a different way. Prior to the Cross, the practical issues were all about the sacrifice — what, how, who, and how many goats covered grand theft? On our side, the practical concern is *experiencing* forgiveness, quite removed from the effectual carnage. This is the felt need of this lesson for Peter, and for every Christian following. Here is what the lesson contains:

### Confession

Notice, first, that Jesus asks Peter "Do you love me?" He asks *three* times, so this clearly has something to do with Peter's three-fold denial, but what exactly?

On the surface it seems almost cruel, like berating a pet who has gone to the bathroom on the carpet. What did you do? But that's not what's happening here, quite the opposite. Jesus is giving Peter the opportunity to say "I love you" for every time he denied him; he is helping Peter to process, digest, and metabolize forgiveness through the act of confession.

The etymology of the Greek word for "confession" literally means "to say the same thing along with someone else," in other words, "to agree" with them. In context it means to agree with God about our sin, which seems strange because, like, why wouldn't we agree? Well if you think about it, when we rationalize or justify our sin, that's exactly what we're doing. Our conscience, confronted with our guilt, responds with a not-so-humble *Yeah... but: but it wasn't my fault; but my blood sugar was low; but I'm a middle child...*" *"Yeah, but"* isn't really agreeing.

So in confessing our sin, we are, first of all, agreeing with God that it's wrong. Second, we are agreeing with God that our sin is forgiven, not because we deserve it or because we feel really bad about it, but because Jesus' death paid for it. The active ingredient of confession is not begging, or manipulating, or excessive sorrow, but faith; we choose to trust in God's forgiveness already given us in Christ.

I know faith can seem nebulous, but we can act upon it concretely. For example, when you've confessed your sin and you still feel that God is angry with you, you can take a passage like Lamentations 3:22-23 (*Because of the Lord's great love we are not consumed, for his compassions never fail. They are new every morning; great is your faithfulness*) and say to the Lord, "I choose to believe the truth, Lord, that you are full of mercy, even though my emotions are telling me something different."

## Confessing Sexual Sin

There's an urban myth claiming chocolate is bad for a dog. Only this is not a myth because you really shouldn't. Dogs don't have an enzyme for digesting chocolate, so they don't, they get sick. Maybe we're missing an enzyme for sexual sin because it's ridiculously hard to metabolize forgiveness. I think I could confess robbing a bank and sleep rather soundly, but not if I visited imagesthatarebadformysoul.com. Maybe it's the shame or the repeated failure or the resolve with which I committed to never do it again; whatever it is, it's different.

The way the legal mind of our conscience handles guilt is to assign punishment: we beat ourselves up until it's paid off like doing community service or something. Then, and only then, when we feel the debt has been worked off, will we allow God's forgiveness. This is not what Jesus wants. He did the punishment part for us, so it doesn't make him happy to see us trying to pay the bill. In fact it's a bit of a toss-up as to what might make him sadder: our sin, or not accepting his payment for it. What he wants us to do is what he wanted Peter to do: confess.

Two, ten, twenty times per day; whenever your conscience prompts you, stop and confess. Don't keep going or make a mental note to try harder. Stop, pause, and confess. Agree with

God about your sin, agree with God that Jesus paid for that sin and that you are forgiven, and then get back to walking in fellowship with him. Confessing your sin throughout the day, when it occurs, as many times as it occurs, is revolutionary to the Christian life. You should really do it.

## Sin Beneath the Sin

Assuming you have read the gospels at one point or another, you'll remember that prior to Jesus' arrest, Peter declares to Jesus (and the other disciples) that even if "all will fall away because of you, I will never fall away (Matthew 26:33). This is not just a declaration of love or loyalty, though it certainly is that; it's a claim to *greater* devotion than the other disciples.

This is why, in their conversation on the beach, Jesus asks Peter: "do you love me more than these?" Clearly Peter felt guilty, but for what, exactly? No doubt for denying Jesus, but that wasn't where the evening went off the rails. The point of departure was clear back when Peter declared himself incapable of moral failure. Peter's denial was merely the result, and an inevitable one, because carrying the Cross is torture, and at some point everyone breaks. For Peter to arrive at restoration, he needed to get to the sin beneath the sin. And there usually is one.

As our focus is sexual purity, pornography is a great example of sin-beneath-the-sin. Sure, sometimes an image just catches your eye like a fish hook and click leads to click and that's all there is to it — just hunger for red meat. But the drive, the compulsion, the habit of turning to porn, has underlying causes: maybe you are not involved in fellowship, maybe you shouldn't be up so late, maybe this is how you handle negative feelings, or maybe you turn to it out of loneliness or detachment. Sometimes "God, I'm sorry I looked at pornography" is tantamount to Peter's "Sorry, I denied you." It's a problem, but it's not *the* problem. Under the habit is a heart.

Failure is not the worst thing in the world, you know. Not even close. Failure is how we grow, how we learn, and how we discover the holes in our hearts. Surface failures make us aware of empty cavities below, and as you confess your sin, make an honest inquiry with the Lord about what's really going on.

## Confessing to Other

Can you imagine how helpful it must have been for Peter to see Jesus: his face, his expressions, his eyes, his kindness? It's hard to feel forgiven when you're the only one in the room, the only one in your head.

James 5:16 says to "confess your sins to each other and pray for each other so that you may be healed." To confess means to face another person, and that person is called to not only be Jesus' hands and feet, but in this case, his face. We need forgiveness incarnated. Jesus has given us his body because you need a warm body. Getting sin out in the open neutralizes its power, severing it from the self-absorption and self-condemnation that gives it life, long after the event.

Technology has come with a price, and with it, there's much to lament and whine about, but also with technology, it couldn't get any easier to confess our sins to each another. Feeling a whole lot better is a simple text: "Dude, I screwed up last night." It helps, it really does. And do it right away. Confess to God, confess to a friend, and regurgitate the sin right away so it doesn't make you sick.

## Comparison

There's something I want you see in the passage that might not seem related but kind-of is:

> Then he said to him, "Follow me!" Peter turned and saw that the disciple whom Jesus loved was following them. (This was the one who had leaned back against Jesus at the supper and had said, "Lord, who is going to betray you?") When Peter saw him, he asked, "Lord, what about him?"

Jesus answered, "If I want him to remain alive until I return, what is that to you? You must follow me."
John 21:19-22

We each have our own race to run in the Christian life, but it's tempting to watch and compare with the race going on in the lane next to ours. Peter, having been dealt with personally by Jesus, wants to know about God's plans for his friend, John. Jesus' response? It's none of your business.

Our experience of forgiveness is muted by our comparison to others' experiences. When we see others failing in the same area, with apparent immunity, we feel we can slack off when God wants us to feel conviction. Conversely, we can look at the lives of Christians around us and paste together a composite of the perfect Christian, causing us to be disheartened in our own growth.

No one knows what sin you have come out of, what stress you endure, what holes exist in your heart, the individual appeal of any particular temptation, and what area of your life God wants to change next. You have a unique race to run, very different from the person in the next lane over. Comparison steals from our experience of forgiveness. As Jesus says to Peter, your job is to "follow" and when you fall, confess, repent, and get back in the race.

## WHY WE ABSOLUTELY HAVE TO GET THIS

The human cell is a thriving community, boasting of a large indigenous population of mitochondria. The problem is that mitochondria have a really fast lifecycle, so they are dropping dead all over the place. The streets of your cells look like streets in the Bronx where cars are left abandoned wherever they stopped working: under a bridge, a parking lot, the middle of the road. Not to worry, our cells have a top-notch sanitation system. Day and night, autophagosome are out and about removing dead mitochondria and taking them to cell's garbage dumps, the lysosomes, where they're hacked up and used for spare parts within

**25**

the cell.

But something strange happens when we get old. The autophagosome stop doing their job, or, more accurately, stop doing it well. They carelessly go right past the dead mitochondria with a mere shrug of their autophagosome shoulders, while murmuring, "Meh." Basically, we die of a garbage strike. The dead mitochondria bodies just keep piling up and our cells look like the living room of a hoarder.

It's not much different in towns and communities in many parts of the world where the sanitation runs like a river through the middle of town. Garbage is always the death of us. Actually, that's not true; poor sanitation is always the death of us, and that's true spiritually as well. The Cross is the ultimate garbage dump for spiritual garbage, as is Gehenna, for those who would reject the former. Gehenna refers to an area outside ancient Jerusalem called Valley of the Son of Hinnom. This is the cursed area where pagans sacrificed children to idol gods. This geographical area is the physical equivalent to the place where the sins of man are left to die.

So here's where I'm going with all this: Two, three, four years from now, if you are not walking closely with the Lord, the reason will not be because of sin, but because of a failure to process that sin, a failure to metabolize forgiveness. The bodies pile up until we don't want to be around other Christians or Jesus.

Dealing with sexual sin — past, present and future — requires a conscious effort to continually take out the garbage, confessing whenever you sin, confessing to other believers, not allowing it the chance to turn toxic in our souls.

### A Little Exercise

As I mentioned earlier, not actually feeling relief for our sin contributes to the struggle to feel forgiven. So sometimes doing something tactile can help. Try this: write all of your sins on a piece of paper. Then, send them to me (just kidding). Confess each one to God as you write them.

Then, write out God's promise found in 1 John 1: 9 across the list:

If we confess our sins, he is faithful and just and will forgive us our sins and purify us from all unrighteousness.

Now, crumple it up.

## Reflection

We are forgiven due to Christ's death for our sin. This is merely an exercise to help experience that forgiveness. When you are struggling to experience forgiveness, what's another practical thing you could do?

Is there someone with whom you can verbally process your struggle, your temptation, your forgiveness?

# BOREDOM

### THE ROOT OF MOST EVIL

*The Screwtape Letters*, written by C.S. Lewis, is a fictional (obviously) correspondence from one demon to another, an uncle (Screwtape) to his nephew (Wormwood), a master tempter to a young protégé. Uncle Screwtape's missives provide Wormwood, and more importantly the reader, with insight into the Enemy's methods of temptation. On the matter of sexual sin, Screwtape advises his nephew thusly:

> "My dear Wormwood ... I have always found that the trough (boring) periods of the human undulation provide excellent opportunity for all sensual temptations, particularly those of sex. The attack has a much better chance of success when the man's whole inner world is drab and cold and empty."

There is an undeniable connection between boredom and sexual temptation and I'm sure you've experienced it. Scripture makes that connection explicit in the account of David's sin with Bathsheba:

> One evening David got up from his bed and walked around on the roof of the palace. From the roof he saw a woman bathing. The woman was very beautiful, and David sent someone to find out about her. The man said, "Isn't this Bathsheba, the daughter of Eliam and the wife of Uriah the Hittite?" Then David sent messengers to get her. She came to him, and he slept with her.
> 2 Samuel 11:2-4a

Cleary on display in the story is the causal chain of David's sin: David planned the death of Bathsheba's husband, Uriah, *because* David got Bathsheba pregnant, *because* David lusted after Bathsheba, *because* David saw Bathsheba taking a bath, *because* David was wandering alone on the rooftop late at night, *because* "In the spring of the year, the time when kings go out to battle, David sent Joab" instead of going himself.

The text seems to imply that David should have been off at war and busy in battle, but he wasn't. Instead he was home with too much time, too little work, no accountability, and the freedom to go anywhere and do anything he wanted. If you think about it, this isn't a bad description of many people's interaction with the internet. No sir, not a bad description at all. On the web, every man is king, and anyone can have a harem.

See, the thing about a causal chain is if you remove just a single link, the result fails to happen. What would have happened if David wasn't bored, or wasn't by himself, or wasn't up on the roof? Probably nothing, and considering what happened, *nothing* would have been a really good outcome.

Circumstances and state of mind (including boredom) are critical links in the chain of events leading to sexual sin. From the perspective of causal necessity, it may have been too late for David to turn back once he saw Bathsheba bathing, but he certainly had the freedom of will and clarity of thought to stop himself from going up on the roof.

### The Riveting History of Boredom

If you're looking for boredom in the Bible, try reading the genealogies in Deuteronomy. If you're looking for the word "boredom" you won't find it; about the closest thing to this is "idleness" which can be boredom (an interior state of mind) viewed from the outside. In her book, *Boredom: The Literary History of a State of Mind*, Patricia Spacks locates 1864 as the birth of modern boredom, or more accurately, the first known use of the word "boredom" in the English language. The word comes to us from French writers who used the word "*ennui*" to refer to "disquiet, tedious, wearisome, or discontentment." Pascal wrote, for example, "man's condition is that of boredom [ennui] and anxiety ... no matter how happy a man may be, if he lacks distraction and has no absorbing passion or pastime to keep boredom away, he will soon get depressed and unhappy."

With or without a word to describe it, people have been bored for a long time — much farther back than 1864. But only in this modern era has boredom become such a dominant sociological issue affecting millions. It may be due to an increase in leisure time, or income, or entertainment options. There's probably a million reasons, but as author Reinhardt Kuhn put it: "It [boredom] is not one theme among others; it is the dominant theme... a modern plague."

By "modern plague," Kuhn means that the common-cold boredom experienced throughout human history has become a virus: a more deadly, virulent, life-numbing strain, broadly infecting the masses. This is not situational boredom, but psychological boredom for which there is no distraction. It's a who cares — everything sucks — nothing matters — let's make a pipe bomb — kind of boredom, and it spawns an apathy and cynicism so extreme as to extinguish all light and life. A truly black hole of negativity.

### What Makes Us Bored?

This new, extreme form of cultural boredom was described with impressive articulation by a group of teens from New York's Greenwich Village, interviewed in a *Time* magazine article. Nineteen-year-old Harry Siegel said this:

> The ability to howl at the moon is lost. The counterculture has been absorbed by the culture. The blue hair and pierced nipples are trite, and no one pays them any mind. Nothing is outside the fold: there's nothing to do but entertainment: make it or watch it.

That kid should definitely be *making* it; that's a heck of line. But I wonder what you see when you look at the culture and where you see it headed? Below are some of the more obvious influences (obvious enough that I've observed them) that contribute to our sense of restlessness, boredom, and discontent. The list is just to get you thinking because I want you to add to it and think of those factors that are influencing you.

## 1. Wealth
The average workweek used to be 55 hours; it's way less that now. Our relative wealth gives us all kinds of free time to fill as we please.

## 2. Technology
The stimulus of technology works like a drug. Life seems boring so we play with our iPhone, which ironically intensifies boredom by increasing the need for stimulus and decreasing our threshold for boredom. The cycle is self-perpetuating.

## 3. Godlessness
With the rejection of God comes a loss of meaning and purpose. Those nagging "why" questions that motivate us are left unanswered. Audrey Fellows writes: "In a world where the reality of things no longer gives life, intense experience is all we have left. There is only intensity; some things feel better than others."

## 4. Tolerance
Dorothy Sayers once said this about tolerance: "In the world, boredom is called tolerance, but in hell it is called despair ... it is the sin that believes in nothing, cares for nothing, seeks to know nothing, interferes with nothing, enjoys nothing, hates nothing, lies for nothing, and remains alive because there is nothing for which it will die."

## 5. Isolation
Most any activity becomes boring and tedious when it is done alone. Isolation brings with it a need to compensate for the lack of relational stimulus. Furthermore, isolation makes us extremely self-centered in our thoughts, causing us to seek distraction and self-gratification.

**FLESH**

So what did I miss? What would you add to these five?

Now, the more important questions: What makes you bored? What do you do when you feel bored?

### Whose Fault Is It That I'm Bored?

Richard Winter, in his book, *Still Bored in a Culture of Entertainment*, writes that up until the modern era, boredom, or the inability to keep one's interest or engagement in the world, was seen as a character flaw linked to one of the Seven Deadly Sins known as *sloth*. Winter writes, "Sloth is the lack of spiritual resources that enable one to appreciate and engage with the common wonders of creation, culture, and people."

Particularly insightful is Winter's observation about blame-shift; when we're bored we no longer probe our own soul by asking, "What is wrong with me?" Instead, we point an irritated finger at the world — the system, the bureaucrats, the 9-5 — that ceaselessly spoil our fun and thwart the exciting adventure that is supposed to be our lives. It simply never occurs to us that our appetite is jaded, our coping skills are underdeveloped, and we are not owed a riveting adventure by virtue of joining the human race. I think there's something spiritually significant in the realization that boredom and dissatisfaction are a spiritual problem, a problem with us and not the world.

### Our Liability

"Because the comfort's so appealing, The bodies so revealing, just get to feeling like a wheel without traction, Stupefaction." – "Stupefaction" by Graham Parker

Immersed in a paradoxical culture of staggering boredom and relentless entertainment, when we come to Christ, our accumulated restlessness does not simply vanish. We have a large and jaded appetite for sensation and this makes the challenge of purity doubly difficult because we have more opportunity and options available, coupled with an appetite two to three times what it should be. It's not too dissimilar to the cultural problem of obesity where an infinite supply of junk conspires against overstretched stomachs and appetites.

Pornography carries with it a *rush* of excitement, both chemically and emotionally, and that rush is immediate relief from boredom. For many guys, boredom was what led them to pornography in the first place and remains a delicate trigger offering a quick, easy fix to boredom, depression, and any other undesirable feeling.

The connection between boredom, sexual sin, and temptation means that the battle for purity will, at some level, involve a battle against boredom. So how do we learn, if we were never taught or never tried, to cultivate an internal capacity for boredom? How do we recapture wonder, passion, and curiosity when those receptors are dulled from over-stimulation? Well, this too is part of our transformation in Christ. Purity, discipline, contentment, industriousness: these things — and many more — are joined symmetrically and grow symmetrically (growth in one is tied to growth in another). So, the question is: what can we do to engage with God on this issue of boredom? As you're prayerful, I trust God's Spirit will lead you to very specific applications. Here are a few generic steps to get you moving in the right direction:

### Repentance

I suppose no one breaks down weeping over time logged in a vegetative state, though if we ever tallied up the hours, actually saw the number, I'm sure it would evoke some kind of emotion. But repentance is, strictly speaking, the acknowledgement of a wrong direction and an intentional change of course. Weeping isn't a part of the definition. So repentance, of a sort, seems in order. We decide to make different choices with our time and attention.

So, for example, if there is a choice between isolating your-self or engaging in community, choose community. When the reason for not doing something seems to be laziness, do it, do it just because. When you have spent large amounts of time on leisure, confess it. You are a steward before God of the time you have been given. Confession and awareness of sin should not be limited to the time spent on evil things but also wasted time and wasted opportunities to engage in the good we could have done (sins of omission).

### Embrace Boredom

We have spent our lives, most of us, running from boredom, dancing as fast as we can to avoid the alternative. But God has great purpose in boredom and we need it for what it alone can teach us. Boredom is the problem, but it is also the cure.

Friedrich Nietzsche wrote: "For thinkers and all sensitive spirits, boredom is that disagreeable 'windless calm' of the soul that precedes a happy voyage. They have to bear it and wait for its effect on them."

Boredom is an impetus to action. It's much like anger — without its fuel, we would not do or say things that need to be done and said. But here is what needs to change: rather than medicating or entertaining our boredom away, we need to cultivate active creative alternatives. They include: creative things, thoughtful things (what you can do to stimulate your mind such as reading or writing), relational things (who you can interact with in order to stimulate social and emotional connections), natural things (what you can do that will put you out in nature), athletic things (what you can do to stimulate your body, not relax it).

These are the healthy directions our minds would go if we weren't raised by iPhones. It is not too late to start. Unlike media, these things replace boredom, but at the same time, they also expand our capacity for boredom. This allows us to use boredom as an impetus for creative doing, which in turn further develops the mind.

### Praise and Wonder

I have found long walks, during which I praise and thank God for the most mundane of things, to regenerate a sense of wonder. I tell God he's a genius for making grass, and I ask him (not expecting an answer) how he conceived of this natural carpet. Praise and thanksgiving give rise to praise and thanksgiving an octave higher. It's an altered state of mind, or it is the return to sanity from a mind altered by technology. Slowly, surely, I find myself excited by things that should excite and bored by things that pass for entertainment.

### Summary

Boredom is a thing. It's a thing in and of itself. It has ties to sexual sin and temptation and so we need to be aware of its power and influence. We need to recognize it. We need to be proactive in dealing with its effects upon us. Like all areas of challenge, we need it to become a trigger to pray and not the alternative. We need to view passivity and laziness as something serious enough to confess to the Lord. And we need to cultivate new, creative, and active habits to replace the easy passive response of sensual stimulation.

# THE PATH OF SPIRITUAL GROWTH

## WHAT WE LEARN — AND DON'T LEARN —
## FROM THE EXAMPLE OF ISRAEL

I paused recently on one of those Dr. Phil-type shows to observe all the pageantry of glamorous dysfunction. The family, or maybe let's call them relatives, were all at one another's throats calling each other horrible things and exchanging accusations about sleeping with one other. I didn't catch the full story, so it's possible they were a team of scientists sharing the results of a 20-year longitudinal study on crazy. Anyway, they had tried every possible method of self-help, but as was abundantly clear, they were just getting worse. So, here they were on Dr. Something, hoping that he would instantaneously fix them, erasing 20 years of destructive behavior in and hour (minus commercial breaks, of course).

There's a dynamic here that's not unfamiliar. It involves the question of spiritual growth and transformation and who exactly is responsible for fixing us. Are we responsible, or is God? Like that family, we oscillate between frenzied self-help and passive helplessness: "fix me, God, fix me."

In 1 John 3:2 there's a brief but beautiful description of our future hope that goes like this: "Beloved, we are God's children now, and what we will be has not yet appeared; but we know that when he appears we shall be like him, because we shall see him as he is. When we see him we will be like him." The promise is of immediate glorification in the presence of Jesus, and it affirms what we already suspected: God can fix us anytime he likes. That being so, God clearly has purpose in our participation, and in the process, he has purpose in our growth and transformation. See, the goal of growing someone is very different than the goal of fixing them.

So, this reframes things a bit. First, we should notice that our goal is to grow in purity, not to be healed of lust. Second, we should see spiritual growth as a partnership between us and the Lord — a collaborative effort in which we collaborate with him in our sanctification. Working collaboratively is a different way of working and it takes getting used to. It's not a neat division of labor.

I want to go back a bit in time, about 3,400 years. Picture the Israelites standing on the east bank of the Jordan River staring across at the Promised Land. Following their Exodus from Egypt, they'd been wandering in the desert for the past 40 years, but now, finally, they were poised to take possession of the "land given them by God."

But what does it mean that the land was "promised" and "given to them by God"? I would have imagined it meant a vacant lot. I would have imagined that God would have informed the inhabitants to move out leaving their domiciles vacant and unoccupied. Upon discovering that the current tenants had no intention of leaving, I suppose I would have asked God for clarity on the phrase "land given us by God." By that definition, Vietnam was "given" us by God.

Then, I suppose it would have dawned on me, or I would have pieced it together that "taking possession of the land" was going to be a collaborative effort, something done together. And indeed it was. In the strictest sense, the land was neither given by God nor taken by Israel, but both together, and only together.

The taking of Canaan is a very helpful — and accurate — picture of our sanctification. At times our sanctification seems as "given us" as the Promised Land, and as a partnership, it's not so clear who is supposed to be doing what. We want to learn from Israel, with the Promised Land as our model, as we continue ahead.

### The Importance of the Process

Take a look at these passages and what God tells Israel about the process of taking the land:

> I will send my terror ahead of you and throw into confusion

> every nation you encounter. I will make all your enemies turn
> their backs and run ... But I will not drive them out in a single
> year, because the land would become desolate and the wild
> animals too numerous for you.
> Exodus 23:27, 29

> When the LORD your God brings you into the land he swore
> to your fathers ... be careful that you do not forget the LORD,
> who brought you out of Egypt, out of the land of slavery.
> Deuteronomy 6:10-12

> You may say to yourself (after you have entered the land),
> My power and the strength of my hands have produced this
> wealth for me.
> Deuteronomy 8:17

Haven't you ever thought, "Why doesn't God just change me
already?" I think the reasons are similar to the reasons he didn't
give Israel the land all at once: You'd forget the enslaving power
of sin, in time you'd believe you had the capacity to change yourself, you wouldn't learn to rely and depend on God, you wouldn't
use your new freedom responsibly, you wouldn't actively engage
in your spiritual growth, you would never fully appreciate what
you'd been delivered from, you would be far less thankful... and
the list goes on.

The result of purity handed to us, without the accompanying
process of growth, would be spiritual privation, the same sort of
result you'd get from giving an 18 year-old a Ferrari for his birthday. For our own good, the effort has be collaborative.

When God says, "But I will not drive them out in a single year,
because the land would become desolate, and the wild animals
too numerous for you..." I think we can picture the analogous
spiritual result. Every victory over temptation yields wisdom,
knowledge, and strength for the next battle; every loss teaches
about grace, humility, prayer and perseverance.

There is inestimable value in the process, but that's not to say
that God has placed victory out of reach. He hasn't.

### Unseen Influence

The book of Joshua is the account of the land's conquest, and it provides a variety of instances of collaboration between God and his people. In each instance, the partnership — what God does and what we do — looks a little different. It's a changing dynamic as all living partnerships are. I want to look at a handful of these dynamics to see the partnership in practice. The result, I hope, will be a better understanding of how we partner with God in our sanctification. So here's the first dynamic:

At the battle of Jericho, the prostitute Rahab informs the Jewish spies of God's Spirit at work. "I know that the LORD has given this land to you," says Rahab, because "a great fear of you has fallen on us, so that all who live in this country are melting in fear because of you" (Joshua 2:9).

Unseen and unnoticed, God's Spirit was working in the hearts and minds of Israel's enemies, and because it was unseen, they would have had no idea God was doing it. I don't think anyone in Israel was thinking, "I bet God is at work making our enemies feel really, really scared of us." So much of God's work is unseen and that's true in our sanctification. Notice what this passage in Philippians says:

> Therefore, my dear friends, as you have always obeyed — not only in my presence, but now much more in my absence — continue to work out your salvation with fear and trembling, for it is God who works in you to will and to act according to his good purpose.
> Philippians 2:12-13

Unseen, God's Spirit is at work in us, "willing" us to "act according to his good purposes." And, because it's a partnership, we also have a role; it is our job to work out what God is working in us. There's a rhythm playing in our hearts and we're supposed to dance.

### Internal Cooperation

Now you might be thinking, "Yeah, I experience God's influence in my life, but the influence of my flesh is just as strong and sometimes even stronger." And that may be true, but this being a partnership means there's something you can do about it. When the apostle Paul says to Timothy "fan into flame the gift of God that is in you," he is telling him to do those things that cultivate the Lord's presence and power in his life. We can't silence the flesh but we can amplify the Spirit.

In Ephesians chapter five when Paul encourages the Ephesians to "be filled with the Spirit," he follows that instruction with the following words:

> Addressing one another in psalms and hymns and spiritual songs, singing and making melody to the Lord with your heart, giving thanks always and for everything to God the Father in the name of our Lord Jesus Christ...
> Ephesians 5:18–20

This is how we are "filled" or "fan into flame" the presence of the Lord in our life. Described are the things that we can do daily to create an atmosphere in our heart that intensifies the Spirit's influence and amplifies his voice. This is something we do, not something God does for us.

### Obedience

Returning to Jericho, to prepare for battle, Israel was given the significant "tactical op" of doing laps around the city. It seems pointless but the pointlessness has a point — a couple of them: first, faith is an internal working that requires outward action to ratify and fortify it; and second, while faith and obedience are indispensable to the battle, only God can give victory.

There's a similar call to manual cooperation in that Philippians passage we looked at: "Continue to work out your salvation with fear and trembling, for it is God who works in you to will and to act according to his good purpose" (Philippians 2:12-13). Obviously, there is a word-play between "working in" and "working out," e.g. we need "work out" or "put into action" the internal working of God.

It is through willful actions and choices that godliness is habitualized in our flesh. Ingrained. This is our role in sanctification, making "right choices" to act out what God is working in us. As it relates to purity, this involves choices to avoid compromising circumstances (choices not to go online, not to be by ourselves), to be transparent with struggles, to be honest about failure, and I'm sure you can think of many others.

## Surge

You can read the book of Joshua in a brisk forty-five minutes, which gives the illusion of a brisk war. Brisk, it was not. Israel's fight for possession of the land was like the endless wars fought in Iraq and Afghanistan: setbacks, small gains, victories, losses, and many lost lives. Israel lost heart. They would fight for a while and then settle for shared occupation with the enemy. All too similar to our sanctification, right? And when they shrunk back, God pushed forward:

> So Joshua said to the people of Israel, "How long will you put off going in to take possession of the land, which the Lord, the God of your fathers, has given you?"
> Joshua 18:3

He pushes us too, not letting us shrink back or settle for mediocrity. The apostle Paul, in his letter to the Thessalonians, says, "like a father with his children, we exhorted each one of you and encouraged you and charged you to walk in a manner worthy of God, who calls you into his own kingdom and glory" (1 Thessalonians 2:12). This is how God pushes.

Fresh vision, encouragement, rest, new motivation: this is something God does for us. We assume it's our job to psyche ourselves up to follow God, but it's not. Counterintuitively, our part is to repent and put our hearts in a place to be comforted and renewed. When you lose heart, settle for mediocrity, or acquiesce to defeat, simply repent. Humble yourself before God, confess the state of your heart, and ask for fresh wind and fresh fire.

## Discipline

One would assume that having entered the land, Israel's days of bondage and slavery were gone forever. That would be a wrong assumption:

> Again the Israelites did evil in the eyes of the LORD, and for seven years he gave them into the hands of the Midianites. Because the power of Midian was so oppressive, the Israelites prepared shelters for themselves in mountain clefts, caves and strongholds.
> Judges 6:1-3

God disciplined Israel... a lot. That kind-of sums up the Old Testament, doesn't it? This discipline often took the form of enslavement because bondage teaches very unforgettable lessons. One of my favorite ads that I think shows the enslaving nature of sin was put out by MADD (Mothers Against Drunk Drivers). The visual is a half-poured drink sitting next to a bottle of alcohol. The copy runs behind the glass in a list, finally disappearing into the drink:

> This drink cost: $2.95... a marriage... a car... two children... a house...

Bondage causes us to despise our master and brings to a boil our passion for freedom. Through bondage, God builds in us the passions and drives that freedom will require. Bondage is just one of many ways that God disciplines us for our good.

## Summary

The fight for your holiness is a partnership. Each battle is different, but we've looked at some of the major ways this partnership plays out. There are other nuances, to be sure, but if you get your mind around these, it will explain a great deal of what you have experienced in your battle for purity. Your continuing battle will teach you further dynamics and dimensions of this partnership. It's like learning to dance. As you grow, you'll pick up the rhythms of the partnership.

# THE WORKS OF FAITH

## WHY SPIRITUAL VICTORY IS DETERMINED BY FAITH, NOT DISCIPLINE

In Ephesians, when Paul gives instructions to "put on the full armor of God," he's of course alluding to the fact that we are in a battle, but there's something else he's communicating through the concept of armor. Armor isn't merely protection, it is multiple, overlapping shields of defense. It's a defensive network.

Dr. John Arquilla is professor of Defense Analysis at the US Naval Postgraduate School and a leading expert on modern warfare and the tactics of terrorist networks. In an interview, Arquilla commented that, "the War on Terror is actually the first great war in which we are seeing nations at war with networks." Arquilla goes on to describe how the US military learned from Afghanistan and Iraq that the way to fight a network is with a network:

> The United States initially approached things in very traditional ways: overwhelming force, massive deployments, and shock and awe. Several years into the war, we moved our soldiers from huge bases to hundreds of small outposts thirty to fifty soldiers apiece, dramatically expanding the number of nodes on our physical network.

Evil is an organized network and the way to fight a network is with a network. And that's the approach we've taken to lust. We must explore the network of defenses given us by God. In this article we'll look at faith's substantial contribution to the battle. Faith is a shield, or more accurately, a network of biblical truths held rigid by active trust.

Faith is trusting in God and the truths that he has communicated to us in his Word. Faith is a resolve, flexed like a bicep, to turn a deaf ear to countering thoughts and feelings. We must lean into the truth and seize upon any opportunity to tangibly act upon that truth.

I just created that definition, but I think it's right; I don't frown when I reread it. That description of faith applies to all areas of our Christian life, but the truths we cling to and the voices we ignore change in light of the struggle. This is the purity struggle, coming after struggles that start with an "o" and before those that begin with a "q." What follows is the network of truths particular to fighting this battle.

### Faith in our Forgiveness

Few of life's great battles are ever won overnight, so in fighting lust, you've no doubt had your nose rubbed in defeat more than once. It feels awful, I know. Nothing is worse than waking up to a hangover of lust's regret, guilt, and shame. And the worst part is knowing it's not going away in a few hours. Sex and impurity leave stubborn stains. A quick word of confession can whisk away most things from our conscience but not this ugly grass stain. Feeling cleansed from the filth and flesh of sexual sin requires a greater application of faith.

This application of faith stands in contrast to psychologizing our guilt away. Here's what I mean by that.

The guilt we heap on ourselves is our way of paying the price of forgiveness, and only when we feel it's been paid will we allow God's forgiveness to rest upon us. It's like we're out to dinner with Jesus and when the check comes, he reaches for his wallet but we grab the check: "Hey, you always pay, let me get this one." It's a nice gesture but we have nothing to pay with and the bill was already paid.

Here's another way we psychologize ourselves: rather than flexing our will in the form of faith, we flex it in the form of commitment, vowing to never do again whatever it was we did. This helps us feel forgiven, but the basis for that feeling is the vow of holiness: it's really faith in future obedience, not in Christ's atonement for our sin. It's a wrong object of faith and a promise we won't be able to deliver on.

And if you think about it, rationalizing or justifying sin, attempting to obtain the feeling of forgiveness by minimizing or denying the offense, is its own form of psychologizing.

These are the mind games we play, the lengths we go to in order to feel forgiven. God knows all that. And instead, what he wants us to do is to sink our faith into his love and forgiveness. He wants us to be honest about our sin, turn a deaf ear to psychologizing, and stand in faith on Christ alone — God's provision for our cleansing and forgiveness.

### Faith That God Can Make You Holy

As Jesus went on from there, two blind men followed him, calling out, "Have mercy on us, Son of David!"

When he had gone indoors, the blind men came to him, and he asked them, "Do you believe that I am able to do this?"

"Yes, Lord," they replied. Then he touched their eyes and said, "According to your faith will it be done to you."
Matthew 9:27-29

No matter the setbacks, we can never relinquish our grip or our faith-hold on God's desire and ability to lead us to a place of victorious living in the sexual area of our lives. By victorious living I do not mean sinless living, and I know that you know that. But to be clear, I mean living with lust under the general control of our will and God's Spirit, the opposite of which is a cycle of sin management with little time on our feet between falls. Victorious living is somewhere up ahead and God has the power to get us there. Believe it. Never doubt it. Always persevere. Continue moving forward.

I was speaking to a group of men at a conference some years

ago on the topic of sexual purity. The title of my message was "Feeling Forgiven." Before the talk, a student came up to me and said that he had something God wanted him to share with the other men. His message was simple. He told them he had been immersed in lust but was now living with tremendous freedom, and God wanted them to know that the same was possible for each of them. I let his message replace mine because in essence I was preparing them to handle failure. God wants them to plan for victory and believe that holiness is not only possible, but exactly what he wants for them.

### Temptation

Okay, here's another truth for faith to hold on to:

> No temptation has seized you except what is common to man. And God is faithful; he will not let you be tempted beyond what you can bear. But when you are tempted, he will also provide a way out so that you can stand up under it.
> 1 Corinthians 10:13

Everyone is prone to believe that they are unique in their struggle, or iniquity, or capacity for lust, or lack of will power, or all of the above, or best three out of four. There is always some nuance of our sexual pathology that makes us feel alone, hopeless, helpless, and worse than everyone else. But it's not true, and you're not an exception. I mean, you're exceptional, but not in this way.

A friend of mine has some of his worst nights on the internet around Christmas and Easter. I obviously don't know, but I'll bet Satan tempts and targets him on those days just so he'll feel that isolating weirdness: "what kind of a Christian looks at porn on Christmas?" Every sexual deviation imaginable can be found on the web, and yet there's still a need for a "dark web," for all that's unimaginable. All of which to say, "No temptation has seized you except what is common to man."

### Faith That All Things Work for the Good

> And we know that in all things God works for the good of those who love him, who have been called according to his purpose.
> Romans 8:28

This is a really important truth for anyone who has been afflicted by sexual sin, whether caused by others (rape, abuse, exposure, parental infidelity), self-inflicted, or if you were the abuser.

In the world of recyclables, sexual sin is Styrofoam, sitting in the landfill of our past, immune to organic dissolution, and with no value for salvage or resale. This is why faith is required. Sexual sin is not going away on its own.

The gospels tell of only two times that Jesus was utterly "amazed," and both relate to faith. Mark 6:6 says that Jesus "marveled because of their unbelief," but yet he also marveled at the faith of the centurion:

> When Jesus heard this, he marveled and said to those who followed him "Truly, I tell you, with no one in Israel have I found such faith..." And to the centurion Jesus said, "Go; let it be done for you as you have believed".
> Matthew 8:13

God is pleased — even amazed — when we take to him things that are truly, thoroughly, terribly broken, and say, "I trust that you have power enough and compassion enough to fix even this."

In the early 1970s, Boston Harbor was dubbed the "harbor of shame" because every day, two million people's untreated sewage was poured into it. The brew of toxins and E. coli was not only fatal to fish, but if a human fell in, health officials called for a mandatory trip to the hospital for a battery of shots, tests, and screenings. Today, not only can you swim in the water, but you can drink it.

The transformation was the result of the construction of a massive sewage treatment plant on Deer Island, dubbed by historically-minded locals as Fort Poop. Daily, Deer Island transforms roughly 390 million gallons of sewage a day into both drinkable water and gas-powered energy.

Faith functions in a way similar to Deer Island. Faith accesses God's resurrection power that turns sewage to water. Faith is the divinely-energized catalyst. Gasoline is just a smelly combustible fluid unless an engine converts it to mileage. A log can't keep you warm until it's burned and turned to heat. Gas and wood are raw materials that require a catalyst to transform them into light, life, and warmth. That's Faith. It brings to bear God's transforming power, taking useless sludge and transforming it into light and life and warmth.

### Faith in God's Goodness

"For I know the plans I have for you," declares the LORD, "plans to prosper you and not to harm you, plans to give you hope and a future."
Jeremiah 29:11

Going back to the Garden of Eden, prior to the sin of disobedience and inevitably leading up to it, was the sin of distrust. Adam and Eve became convinced that God was "holding out on them," deliberately keeping them from a better, more fulfilling life. If you look hard enough, at the root of most sin is a lack of faith in God's goodness, a distrust that his plans for us are really best.

Life's hardships and stress are the raw materials out of which a justification is formed. We find ourselves thinking, "Why hasn't he found me a girlfriend, or made other areas of my life easier?" We don't necessarily believe these things, but our flesh is looking for permission and we know that dwelling on such thoughts will inevitably cross some threshold of conscience, permitting us to do the unpermitted.

Through difficult and constraining circumstances, our hearts must be cloaked in thanksgiving, which, when life is hard, is something done in faith. Thanksgiving, offered in faith, prevents justifying and entitling thoughts from ever starting a revolution. This isn't happy-talk. This is a conscious choice to ground your mind in the truth, and that truth is that everything God does in your life is motivated by love.

### Faith in God's Goodness Part 2

> God disciplines us for our good, that we may share in his holiness. No discipline seems pleasant at the time, but painful. Later on, however, it produces a harvest of righteousness and peace for those who have been trained by it.
> Hebrews 12:10b-11

It's a rather unfortunate truism that any trial or hardship occurring within the general time frame of lust will be viewed as "payback." It's not, but we'll see it that way. So atop a heap of guilt is added miserable circumstances accompanied by the demoralizing thought that it's God's judgment. This is some seriously screwy thinking because the "payback" was already paid back and the result is what Hebrews 12 tells us: God disciplines (as opposed to punishes) in love (as opposed to anger) for our good (and not God's justice). Because Christ assumed the judgment for our sin, there is no element of retribution, justice, or anger in God's dealings with us — none.

Often, we'll experience the Lord's discipline in our life when all is going well for the very reason that God doesn't want us to see judgment in our trials because it's simply not there. The point is that this is another place where faith must cling to the goodness of God and sufficiency of Christ, and we must turn a deaf ear to thoughts that God is angry or punishing us.

### Our Salvation

In physics, sometimes the principle that comes before all others is not referred to as "first" but as "zeroth" because, well, zero is a also number and it is fully deserving of the honor, rights and privileges of one. Intolerant of any form of numerical discrimination, I shall call the truth of our salvation the zeroth truth proposition, as it is before, behind, and above all other spiritual truths about us.

> Yet to all who received him, to those who believed in his name, he gave the right to become children of God.
> John 1:12

> I write these things to you who believe in the name of the Son of God so that you may know that you have eternal life.
> 1 John 5:13

In describing our spiritual armor, Paul describes the truth of our salvation as a helmet, presumably because it safeguards the mind and defends us from doubt. Protracted, habitual sin, as lust-related sins often are, leads to doubts about our salvation. We naturally start to worry, "Would some people who are truly saved be struggling and failing the way I am?" The answer is "yes", they would. Now please listen to me: if you gave your life to Christ, then you have eternal life. Unsaved people don't worry about not being saved. Fear of losing your salvation indicates your belief in its reality and your desire for it. This is how "saved" people think, not "unsaved." Now enough of that.

## How Faith Grows

Faith is like a muscle and it grows by lifting weights. Weights are the resistance: the doubts, the mental whispers, and the circumstances that tell us the opposite of what through faith we must believe. When God seems to be absent and difficult circumstances swirl around us, everything seems to shout, "God isn't here! If he was, he certainly doesn't care." In those circumstances, faith curls truth toward your heart and says, "No, God is good. He is for me. He has a plan." Thus, it is our circumstances that are adverse to our faith that become the vehicle for our growth.

The struggle with lust and pornography will, at times, lead those inflicted to form the greatest resistance to the truths mentioned above. But as you curl these truths, repetitiously, flab will turn to faith.

## Reflection

Where are you most prone to doubt the goodness of God?

Where do you need to exert the greatest faith right now?

How does your prayer reflect faith?

What is it you fear most about the plan and purposes God may have for you?

How has God shown his goodness and faithfulness to you?

You know you can trust God with every part of your life because...

# TEMPTATION

**There's More to Standing Firm than Standing Firm**

"Yo, yo, little man, come here; I got somethin' for you. It's an article on sex, everyone's reading it — go on, give it a try. Nice, right? Tell your friends who hooked you up, little bro."

I was hoping to entice you into the next topic, which is temptation. But before shifting our focus to evil and temptation, we should acknowledge that Satan is not to blame for every tempting thought that wafts through our heads. We are not only capable, but we are quite proficient in tempting ourselves:

> When tempted, no one should say, "God is tempting me." For God cannot be tempted by evil, nor does he tempt anyone. Each one is tempted when, by his own evil desire, he is dragged away and enticed. Then, after desire has conceived, it gives birth to sin. Sin, when it is full-grown, gives birth to death."
> James 1:13-15

With that said, there is absolutely a demonic dimension to lust, sexual immorality, pornography, and anything that might go under those three headings. We don't want to be ignorant of this aspect of the battle which is what motivated Paul to warn the Christians in Ephesus that our struggle is not "against flesh and blood, but against the rulers, against the authorities, against the cosmic powers over this present darkness..." (Eph. 6:12). If you have an internet problem, you could pound the keys on your keyboard all day and it won't make a difference because the source of the problem is not in the physical keys but in the vast unseen world of cyberspace. However, we do this anyway, just like we treat spiritual problems like they are flesh and blood.

In that same passage, the apostle Paul instructs us to take a stand against the devil's schemes. The Greek word for "schemes" is **noemata** which means "mind or thought." From **noemata** we get our word "noose", and isn't that interesting? The point is that Satan's efforts are strategic — no wasted motion. His intercessions will occur at opportune times, vulnerable times, and vulnerable states (tired, frustrated, isolated, discouraged, anxious, etc.). Satan's strategy requires that we have a strategy of our own, which is what Paul gives to us in the proceeding verses:

> Therefore take up the whole armor of God, that you may be able to withstand in the evil day, and having done all, to stand firm. Stand therefore, having fastened on the belt of truth, and having put on the breastplate of righteousness, and, as shoes for your feet, having put on the readiness given by the gospel of peace. In all circumstances take up the shield of faith, with which you can extinguish all the flaming darts of the evil one; and take the helmet of salvation, and the sword of the Spirit, which is the word of God, praying at all times in the Spirit, with all prayer and supplication. To that end keep alert with all perseverance, making supplication for all the saints...
> Ephesians 6:13-18

That's a lot to take in, so let me try to condense it to a few essential principles.

## Stand Firm

> So that when the day of evil comes, you may be able to stand your ground, and after you have done everything, to stand. Stand firm then...
> Ephesians 6:13–14

No less than three times, the passage tells us to stand firm against the devil's schemes. The awkward phrasing — "stand, after standing, stand firm" — draws our attention to the fact that a passive verb (stand) is being used in a very active way. It would be like a crowd at a football game standing to their feet and roaring: "PLAY DEAD" or "HIBERNATE." Quite intentionally, we find the word "stand" where the text leads us to expect "march."

In his dissertation on *Power and Magic in Ephesus*, Clinton Arnold suggests that this is meant to communicate something important about spiritual battle: that standing our ground is marching forward. I'll explain.

On a map, the Kurram Valley, Orakzai, and North Waziristan are all snugly within the northwest border of Pakistan. As the Pakistani government is an official ally of the U.S. in the war on terror, we could conclude that these regions are free from terrorists. They are not free from terrorists; they are Disneyland for terrorists. Though they lay within the borders, it's a misnomer to say these territories are under the government's control. The enemy is free here to do whatever it wants.

Likewise, we assume that our speech, appetites, thoughts, ambitions, and so forth, are all safely within the borders of our control, and we are controlled by Christ. But this just isn't so. Like in Pakistan, territory owned and territory occupied are two different things. Whenever the enemy can march in at any time and do whatever it pleases, it's just not true to say it's an area under the Spirit's control. And most of us have these areas; areas, that given certain circumstances, we will capitulate to sin with little or no resistance.

When we say no to temptation, we do not simply keep the enemy out, we seize control of the unsecured territories within our own borders. We march forward by standing still. And here we cross paths with one of God's purposes in and through evil. It conscripts us to battle, leaving us no option but to fight. This is how God made an army out of Israel. He let the Philistines move next door, forcing them to fight for their borders.

If we simply stood firm in those areas of lust where we habitually surrender to sin, if we could just hold out once, twice . . . we could establish a border, turn the tide, and redraw the boundary line between evil and us.

### Godly Armor

> Therefore take up the whole armor of God, that you may be
> able to withstand in the evil day. Stand therefore, having fas-
> tened on the belt of truth, and having put on the breastplate
> of righteousness ... take up the shield of faith ... the helmet of
> salvation, and the sword of the Spirit...
> Ephesians 6:13–17

Eat right, drink orange juice, and get exercise. Do these things
and you will live a long healthy life. Oh, and I should mention
that if you don't, you could get sick. This is the basic tenor of the
discourse on spiritual armor.

In previous sections of the letter, Paul has addressed these
same themes (righteousness, truth, faith, and prayer) but with
a positive spin, and from a perspective of spiritual health — do
these things and you will be blessed! But at the end of the letter,
Paul reviews the same topics from the angle of liability: Oh, and
by the way, if you don't do these things, you will leave yourself
open to spiritual attack. Like orange juice, you can drink it to feel
healthy and alive or you can drink it to keep from getting sick.
Either way, drink it.

In coming to the "spiritual armor" section of the passage, it
has always seemed to me that Bible teachers and commentators get overly mired in the military minutiae of Roman warfare.
Whether the Roman breastplate buckled in the front or had
embossed abs like Batman's body suit doesn't address the most
pertinent question. So we're going to skip through the particulars
of the body armor and address that question: what does it mean
to wear this stuff?

### Satan Is a Splinter

Schism is an ugly word, and it stands in contrast to its whole-
grain antonym, integrity. Integrity refers to internal consisten-
cy — wholesome through and through. It is the condition of
being unified, harmonious, and whole, and it is a feature of God's

design found throughout creation.

Schism is the splitting apart or dividing of something created to be whole. Schism is a design principle of Satan's handiwork: evil's corrosive method of disintegrating godly integrity.

When Satan seeks to attack the mind, the cracked doorway is a breach in the mind's integrity. Drugs fragment consciousness, anxiety and fear divide the mind, lies and deceit bifurcate reality, trauma disassociates mind from body, guilt and shame turn the mind against itself, and so on and so forth. The gaps in our integrity are where we are vulnerable to a splinter.

In the realm of relationships there is also an integrity that must be guarded and maintained. Gossip, envy, slander, and a lack of forgiveness sever relational ties, while isolation, rejection, and bitterness single us out and splinter us off. Satan exploits the gaps that compromise the integrity of the community.

In the moral realm, it is our sin and hypocrisy that create the divide, forming a gulf between what we project and who we are, what we say and what we do. The greater the gap between perception and reality, beliefs and actions, truth and lies, the easier it is to splinter.

In the spiritual realm, the integrity of our new identity in Christ is maintained by faith. Vulnerability exists in that gap between what is true of us in Christ and what we functionally believe to be true. We are forgiven, we are God's children, we have eternal life, and God's Spirit indwells us. The extent to which we shrink back and disbelieve is the gap between head and helmet.

Paul's letter to the Ephesians divides neatly in two. Chapters 1–3 are a call to believe rightly and live out our new identity in Christ. Chapters 4–6 are a call to live rightly. As a summary of the letter, the armor of Ephesians 6:13 is a call to "gapless" living in faith and in practice. Putting on the armor means closing the gaps.

It would be good to think about closing the gaps as it relates to sexual purity. Where does Satan get a foothold? Maybe you are vulnerable when you're up late. Closing that gap would be trying to flip your schedule around. Maybe there are gaps in what you watch and what you listen to.

Clearly, we don't live sinlessly — no one's armor fits like spandex. This, rather, is a charge to pursue "gapless living," repent of glaring gaps and gaping holes, and reconcile (confess, forgive) immediately when and where gaps occur, affording Satan nothing to exploit.

### Playing With Weapons

Having done everything to stand firm and defend ourselves, in the last verses of the text, we are handed a weapon. Finally, we get to shoot something:

> And take the helmet of salvation, and the sword of the Spirit, which is the word of God, praying at all times in the Spirit, with all prayer and supplication. To that end keep alert with all perseverance, making supplication for all the saints
> Ephesians 6:17, 18

Of all the people who might presume upon God for special protection, you'd have to put the Apostle Paul — writer of Scripture, apostle to the nations — at the top of that list. And yet, can you think of anyone who took it less for granted? Paul never presumes, he prays. He prays "unceasingly" and bundles in his beefy arms all the kindling of prayer support he can gather.

The reason I didn't set aside time to pray this morning is simple: I presumed upon God's protection and power. I just figured it'd be there in the morning like my breakfast cereal. Of all the reckless behavior observed in this text, prayerlessness may be the costliest. And we'll never know what it cost, what didn't need to be or what might have been. Paul never assumed things would just work out, never assumed God's sovereignty ensured a favorable outcome, never assumed anything, but prayed about everything. I love that about him.

There are so many other things to attend to in the battle against lust that strangely we can fail to pray. What if you prayed specifically about this area, maybe three or four different times a day? What if you committed to this for months or a year? How much effort have you really put into prayer? Prayer is a revolution, and eventually, all strongholds are toppled. Eventually. The statement "I've tried prayer" borders on oxymoronic because it implies that we've stopped and failed to persevere in praying. It means that what we've tried is "non-persevering" prayer, and that very well may not work. Go to the Lord every day, several times a day, for a year or two, and then evaluate what prayer did or didn't do.

In the text, prayer is paired with Scripture, not because they go nicely together (though they do), but because Scripture, like prayer, is an offensive endeavor — a preemptive activity, a drill practiced daily. When the "day of evil" comes, it's too late to open your Bible because power and protection are not in the Bible, they are in the transfer of its truth to our head and heart. Apart from daily intake of scriptural truth, there is no battle, only a beating.

### A Couple of Last Thoughts

There's no question that Satan is strategic, but so is God in his protection and provisions. In facing temptation, Scripture tells us that "God is faithful; he will not let you be tempted beyond what you can bear. But when you are tempted, he will also provide a way out so that you can stand up under it" (1 Corinthians. 10:13).

The promise of a means of escape carries some logical implications. If God provides an exit strategy, it means that standing face-to-face with that particular temptation is beyond our capacity, or most likely so. It means that God's provision for us is through deliverance *from* circumstances, not empowerment *within* those circumstances.

Certain circumstances, on certain days, lead to a dead end. On such days you will notice exit ramps: opportunities to avoid what will become unavoidable. You need to take one of those exits. You'll have just enough willpower for that decision, but probably not for the decision facing you at the end of the road. This is why you're being given an escape route. Take the escape route — get out, don't go, make a call, take a friend, change your plan...exit.

### BE A GOOD LOSER

I know it's odd to end this discussion of spiritual battle with advice on how to lose, but losing battles well is part of winning the war. Losing well means bouncing back from momentary defeats, not letting them demoralize you, and not allowing them to domino into a string of defeats.

When we fall to lust, it's tempting to stay on the ground. Our flesh immediately suggests that "Seeing as we've blown it, we might as well blow it again, because we'll get it all out of our system and then *really* get a fresh start." This is how one lost battle turns into five and how sinful patterns are re-established. If you fall, get right back up. Confess, receive God's forgiveness, spit out the blood, rub your jaw where you got punched, and get up.

### Reflection

What are some of the patterns you've noticed about how and when Satan tempts you?

What does "getting right back up" practically look like for you?

Where is God calling you to stand firm?

What aspect of your armor is the weakest?

Do you have any plans to shore up your defense against spiritual attack?

How often each day are you praying? Do you pray each day for protection and purity?

# TWO OF A KIND

---

## SO YOU'RE ATTRACTED TO THE SAME SEX

I wrote *Flesh* a dozen years ago. This is a revision of the book, but in light of changes in the world, it's turning into a complete rewrite. And no issue marks the change of the past decade more than homosexuality. Much of the change has been political, so much so that in talking about it I want to be very careful to define context. I am assuming you are a Christian whose priority in life (above everything else) is to walk faithfully with the Lord. I'm assuming you believe the Scripture is God's inspired Word. I'm assuming you want to better understand this issue from a biblical perspective and how best to walk with God in light of what Scripture says. If that's not you, then this article is not for you; it will be more frustrating than fruitful. If that *is* you, then read on. There should be some clarity and encouragement in here for you.

Well, there's just a whole lot we *don't* know about homosexuality and I think that's a good place to start. We must humbly admit that we are not in possession of all the facts and factors involved in same-sex attraction. Research from biology and psychology have been far from conclusive, and you'd have to say this research has been driven every bit as much by politics as by science.

But unlike the culture, Christians do have an objective starting point with God's Word. With considerable detail, Scripture presents us with God's design for the sexes, for sex, and for marriage.

Without Scripture, it would be impossible to define normative sexual behavior because "normative" suggests what "normal" people do, and what does that even mean? With the proliferation of sin in the world, who doesn't have aberrant desires and fantasies, such as role playing, domination, voyeurism, fetishism, and the list goes on...for a really, really long time. To define human sexuality by what people find arousing would be to not define it, because what would you exclude? You could probably find someone, somewhere, aroused by Rice Krispies... or aliens... or poinsettias. And yes, it's pretty weird that those are the things that came to my mind, but let's keep moving.

Scripture gives us an objective standard of right and wrong, healthy and unhealthy, life-affirming and life-debasing, and that standard is based upon God's design in creating us, creating marriage, and creating sex. Scripture is silent on many issues (there isn't a whole lot on air safety, for example) but it is articulate on sex, clearly defining how it functions, malfunctions, and dysfunctions.

So what does Scripture tell us about homosexuality? I think maybe the place to start is with the Old Testament and with what Scripture *doesn't* say about homosexuality. Orthodox Rabbi Michael Gold explains an important distinction:

> "An important point to make from the outset is that Jewish law does not teach that it is forbidden to be a homosexual. On the contrary, Jewish law is concerned not with the source of a person's erotic urges nor with inner feelings, but with acts. The Torah forbids the homosexual act, known as *mishkav zakhar*, but has nothing to say about homosexuality as a state of being or a personal inclination. In other words, traditionally, a person with a homosexual inclination can be an entirely observant Jew as long as he or she does not act out that inclination."

God knows the brokenness of his creation. We are all affected, or more accurately, defected. God's commands in the Old Testament never required anyone to pretend to be attracted to the opposite sex. What was forbidden was to live out that brokenness, to animate and display that which was not God's design for sex and marriage.

With that Old Testament context in mind (the distinction between internal proclivity and external conformity) we'll turn to the New. And with a need for brevity, we'll limit ourselves to the most explicit and challenging of New Testament passages: that addressed by Paul to the Romans. The text is as follows:

> They exchanged the truth of God for a lie and worshiped and served created things rather than the Creator, who is forever praised. Amen. Because of this, God gave them over to shameful lusts. Even their women exchanged natural relations for unnatural ones. In the same way the men also abandoned natural relations with women and were inflamed with lust for one another. Men committed indecent acts with other men, and received in themselves the due penalty for their perversion.

With sweeping generalization, Paul describes the godlessness of the Gentile world. While examples of pagan godlessness abound, Paul highlights homosexuality for illustrative purposes. The illustration is as follows: men and women were created to worship God, created with an innate heart-attraction to Him. Sin, however, bent the internal arrow of that attraction and pointed it in the opposite direction toward false gods and the worship of the creation rather than the Creator. It is the twisting of natural attraction (as designed by God) that is in view, and of this, homosexuality is a physical correlative where innate attraction to the opposite sex has been subverted and redirected.

The specific application of the metaphor (what homosexuality is being likened to) doesn't leave room for misconstruing Scripture's view or verdict. Homosexuality is a disfigurement (a bentness or brokenness) of what God designed for sex, intimacy, and marriage. It is a bentness of attraction, and as we reflect our Father in heaven, that bentness is not to be lived out or reflected in our lives. I honestly wish there were some wiggle room here, but there just isn't. This is an ontological, not a cultural, diagnosis, meaning that homosexuality is being presented, in its *essence*, as bent attraction.

Now, those of us who love God and love his Word are more inclined to twist its meaning than outright disobey it. You'd be amazed, for example, at the ways Christians justify marrying a non-believer. When there is a compelling reason to find Scripture unclear, we often will. And finding a seminarian to support that conclusion (any conclusion) is easy enough, like finding a doctor willing to prescribe pain meds. But let's not do that here. God has a wonderful plan for your life, he really does. It will be better than your plan, and the best way forward is to stay within the safety of his Word and his Will. There is no peace or comfort in facing the challenges ahead without that security.

### Of the Many Causes

Because gay rights is a defining social issue, it is very difficult to get to the question of cause. Moralists will often insist that responsibility lies with the individual's "choice" to engage in a homosexual lifestyle. Sadly, this belief can be motivated by a desire to connect cause with blame. Christians can focus on individual choice as well, but for a different reason. A desire to disconnect God from blame allows Christians to wrongly assume that "born that way" infers "made by God that way." The LGBTQ community, on the other hand, will entertain nothing but a biological cause, and there's good reason for that. The label "born that way" implies ideas like right, natural, normal, unchangeable, irreversible, and irresistible. Such ideas and associations are obviously beneficial to their cause. Well, for those struggling with their same-sex attraction, this debate merely adds another layer of confusion.

I honestly don't know how it all fits together, but several things are certain: people are born with all manner of conditions because we are born "broken." A child born with cerebral palsy or an addiction to crack infers nothing about God's design, the child's nature, or her future hope; it infers only the brokenness of the world. Second, God is not concerned with connecting cause to blame, and I can't think of a passage that makes this clearer than John 9:1-3:

> As he passed by, he saw a man blind from birth. And his disciples asked him, "Rabbi, who sinned, this man or his parents, that he was born blind?" Jesus answered, "It was

not that this man sinned, or his parents, but that the works of God might be displayed in him.

Jesus is not interested in debating the cause nor in assigning blame, but he is interested in restoring that which is broken.

In their book *Authentic Human Sexuality*, Dr. Judith and John Balswick suggest an alternative, more integrated model of causation:

> We suggest that an individual must possess, as a necessary contributor, a genetic or hormonal package at birth or through the process of physical maturation that renders a person susceptible to a homosexual orientation ... However, biological factors are insufficient in and of themselves to produce a homosexual orientation. What is further needed is sufficient environmental causes (family, psychological, or social).

According to the Balswicks, if a predisposition is offset with a number of positive environmental factors, then chances are that the individual will develop a healthy, opposite sex attraction. But if the predisposition is met with certain negative factors, influences, and experiences, then it becomes more likely the individual will continue on a path toward homosexuality. There is also a volitional aspect of the process. Many of these individuals will make decisions along the way to engage in homosexual experiences and relationships. These decisions will concretize a "leaning" into action and confirm the same-sex orientation to the mind and body.

To be clear, this is just a model, but in taking to account the complexity of causes — biological, familial, social, spiritual, volitional — it's instructive. Most complex issues have complex causes.

Whatever the process, looking back, it will appear seamless: an imperceptible undertow, an orientation determined at birth. But all of us view our personal history with this same sense of inevitability, described by Malcom Gladwell as "creeping determinism."

"On the eve of Richard Nixon's historic visit to China, the psychologist Baruch Fischhoff asked a group of people to estimate the probability of a series of possible outcomes of the trip. What were the chances that the trip would lead to diplomatic relations? That Nixon would meet with the leader of China, Mao Tse-tung, at least once? That Nixon would call the trip a success? As it turned out, the trip was a diplomatic triumph, and Fischhoff went back to the same people and asked them to recall what their estimates of the visit had been. He found that they now, overwhelmingly, "remembered" being more optimistic than they had actually been. If you originally thought that it was unlikely that Nixon would meet with Mao, afterward, when the press was full of accounts of their meeting, you'd "remember" that you had thought the chances of a meeting were pretty good. Fischhoff calls this phenomenon "creeping determinism" — the sense that grows on us, in retrospect, that what has happened was actually inevitable."

Well, even if we knew the process with absolute surety, that wouldn't change the struggle or burden, the grace needed, nor the cleansing and forgiveness that's offered for every step along the way. And in the remainder of this short article, let me turn to these sorts of issues and give some older-brother advice.

### Christians with Homosexual Orientation

I am not a counselor (maybe that's painfully obvious) so that might be a very fruitful next step. Make sure it's a Christian counselor, someone who takes both the burden of homosexuality and walking with Jesus seriously.

Second, I want to encourage you to share your struggle with other believers — not everyone, but certainly there are several people you can trust. There is grace in getting it out in the open and bringing other believers in. If those in your faith community are not supportive then you need to get out of there and find a faith community that will walk with you on this journey.

There are, and I suppose there always have been, two extremes on the spectrum of faith communities, represented in Scripture by the Pharisees and Sadducees. Pharisees were the legalists with a sense of uprightness that comes from looking down on others. The Sadducees were theologically liberal; their outlook conformed to current politics and culture. Jesus had little patience for either. And so it is today. There are legalistic churches, zealous in their judgment of homosexuality, and liberal churches embracing and encouraging it. Neither is a good option, neither is biblical. As a believer struggling with homosexuality, you need love and encouragement, not judgement. At the same time, any encouragement to pursue this lifestyle would be toxic. You need a faith community passionate about Jesus and faithful to his Word, and unless you live in Alaska, you should find such a place somewhere nearby. Go there.

Third, remember that sin is sin. Acting upon homosexual desires and feelings is no different from any other way we step outside of God's holy will for our lives. Restoration follows the same process: confess your sin to the Lord, by faith receive his forgiveness and cleansing, and turn from your sin (repentance), walking in grace and obedience.

Fourth, don't compare your spiritual journey with others. Seriously, don't. Your struggle with this issue will be similar to others but it will also be different, as will God's unique work of grace in your life. In Corinthians Paul speaks of some unnamed "thorn in the flesh" which he pleads with the Lord to take away:

> A thorn was given me in the flesh, a messenger of Satan to harass me, to keep me from becoming conceited. Three times I pleaded with the Lord about this, that it should leave me. But he said to me, "My grace is sufficient for you, for my power is made perfect in weakness." Therefore I will boast all the more gladly of my weaknesses, so that the power of Christ may rest upon me. For the sake of Christ, then, I am content with weaknesses, insults, hardships, persecutions, and calamities. For when I am weak, then I am strong.

Like Paul, it could be that God's grace will strengthen and

comfort you in a continuing struggle, or perhaps his grace will bring restoration — or some measure of it. Regardless, there will be manifold grace along the path God leads, and that grace will be sufficient. It will not always feel sufficient, as it undoubtedly didn't for Paul, or he wouldn't have been pleading in the first place. But it will be what you need, when you need it, and it will be what is best for you, because God loves you. As Paul and much of Scripture confirms: God's favor is most often reflected in not removing us from tribulation.

Fifth, because our culture is obsessed with sex, it views sexual orientation as central to one's personal identity. It's not. Your identity in Christ is primary and all other identity markers (family, ethnicity, gender, politics, sexual orientation, etc.) are a distant second.

Last, don't feel sorry for yourself. No doubt you've seen *Lord of the Rings* and can summon to mind the image of Frodo with the ring of Sauron draped around his neck. Frodo's task is to bear the burden and carry the ring to its designated end without letting it corrupt or destroy him. If homosexuality is your struggle, then this is the ring you bear and you could, just as easily, have been given another. Everyone has some burden that serves as the crucible (cross) of their spiritual commitment and growth. This could be the death of a child, a difficult marriage, a horrible job, a drug addiction, an abusive spouse, mental illness, poverty, or cancer. Some rings are easier to bear than homosexuality and some are harder. We don't get to choose our burden, but we do get to choose how we'll respond. You can wear the ring and capitulate to its power by your doing; you could bear it resentfully, growing in frustration and bitterness towards God; or you could embrace it as your journey, growing in faith and perseverance as God grows and refines you through this struggle. It's up to you. As a crucible, the struggle will direct your journey, shape your character, and define victory no matter what.

The life of a disciple is one of cross-bearing, of a constant dying to self. Everyone who truly walks with Jesus discovers this. Though Jesus made the cost of following quite clear, it is not clear to many who begin following — not in this country anyway. But those struggling with homosexuality know it from the start, in the way that Christians living in Muslim countries know what it will mean to follow Christ. But make no mistake, the cost is the same for homosexual and heterosexual, for someone living in Syria or Minnesota — it costs everything to be a disciple, and a disciple is willing to pay it.

### Reflection

Who can I talk with about this?

Who do I know and trust that can refer me to a good Christian counselor?

Thank God for the goodness and grace in his unique plan for your life, in your unique struggles, in your salvation, and in the honor of being called as his disciple.

What next steps would God have you take?

What would it mean for you to fully embrace this as a divine crucible, entrusted to you?

# ALONE WITH OUR THOUGHTS

## LIVING WITH THE CURSE OF MASTURBATION

If you know your Bible well, then you already know that it doesn't have much to say on the topic of masturbation. So either I have to make stuff up or this is going to be a very short chapter. I'll make stuff up. But it will be biblical kinds of stuff.

Let's start with that rather remarkable fact that the Bible doesn't talk at all about masturbation. How odd, considering it is one of the most vexing banes of our spiritual existence. Some would say that it is simply subsumed under the broader category of "sexual immorality," while others suggest that Scripture's silence is tacit approval — a biblical policy of don't ask, don't tell. We can look more at that question in a moment, but for now, let's just breathe in the fresh air of this encouragement: the weight biblically assigned to masturbation is drastically out of proportion with the degree of guilt and loathing we experience when we fail and fall.

Seriously, don't you wish you felt half as bad about being unkind or uncaring? What's up with that? Think of all that Scripture has to say about love and how little our conscience is bothered by gross failings to "love one another, deeply from the heart" (1 Peter 1:22). We should take comfort where it can be found, and I think there is a good bit of it in Scripture's silence on this issue. That's not to say it's unimportant or that it's right or that it doesn't serve as an open door to lust, but it is a fact that our conscience is out of alignment with God's heart on the matter. Maybe that's owing to the shame and embarrassment involved with the act, but whatever it's owing to, it is out of alignment.

A godly man who discipled me as a young believer used to say to our men's Bible study that while the Bible doesn't mention masturbation, it's quite clear about lust. He would then say to us, "If you can masturbate without lusting, be my guest." Maybe our Bible study group was particularly gifted in this way, but we found it exceedingly possible. So much for easy answers. I know of a seminary professor who shares with his class that when he travels, he thinks about his wife and sees nothing wrong with masturbation in this context. It's an interesting point which I might ponder further if it didn't bring to mind images of the professor that, frankly, make me never want to have sex again.

So while we have a lack of biblical data, we do have all kinds of perspectives, definitions, loopholes, and exemptions. On top of that, many of us have an overactive conscience that puts masturbation in the same camp as genocide. What are we to do about this? Well, seeing as I'm writing this article, though I'm not an expert on masturbation nor would I want the title "masturbation expert," I will share with you my perspective.

First, I think we're much freer to consider this question when we have the goal set before us of *growing* in purity (moving from one degree to another) as opposed to the goal of attaining purity or not losing our purity. See, if you step back from the New Testament and think about the overall picture it presents of holy and righteous Kingdom living, the self-gratification of masturbation does not seem to resonate with this picture. Sometimes taking a question out of the stark light of "good vs. evil" makes it easier to see. I think, for example, most people could agree to the statement that masturbation is *less* than what God would have for his kingdom people, and he calls us to a life of *greater and greater* purity.

So what makes masturbation less than the ideal of biblical purity? I'm sure you've seen and experienced some of the reasons firsthand: it's a gateway to lust, it's self-absorbing where sex and love are other-centered, it becomes an habitual way of regulating negative emotions, it's a capitulation to momentary weakness, it affects our self-image and confidence, it leaves a residue of uncleanness, and apart from everything else on this grocery list, it affects our intimacy with the Lord, and that really sucks.

The opposite of seeing ourselves as progressively growing in purity is seeing ourselves in a current state of purity until we slip and fall into sexual temptation. But it's doubtful that we're in some kind of cryogenic state of perpetual purity until that moment of masturbation. On any given day, our thoughts, hearts, and minds are all over the place. Masturbation seems to be more of a reflection of the general purity or impurity attending our lives.

When our goal is "growing in purity" and not achieving or losing it, I think we're freer to allow for the relative context of our personal sanctification. If once-upon-a-time you used to masturbate every day, but now it's something you do only now-and-again, well, that's really awesome. Given our context, failure in regards to perfection can still quite accurately be labeled success in terms of growth. "It is true that I failed," and "it is true that I'm growing" are not contradictory statements and can be synonymous. This is a description of the same reality using different measurements (perfection vs. growth).

This path I've mapped out is one of grace and truth. It takes seriously God's call to a very different type of life, one with the highest degree of love, truth, and purity. It doesn't downgrade the vision of holiness to fit in the door our sexualized selves. It doesn't have to. There's grace that allows us to be right where we are, allows for cleansing when we fail, and provides motivation to grow into the fuller freedom, love, and light that is the essence of purity.

### Practical Avoidance

As you grow in purity, it is a significant milestone to get to a place where you're abstaining from masturbation altogether. By "altogether", I mean like a cigarette smoker who has quit (except for the occasional drag on someone else's cigarette), where smoking no longer plays an active role in their life. And this is a place you can get to. And when you've arrived you'll realize that you're still not Jesus-like, and there is even more glorious purity to be gained. But that doesn't mean this isn't an amazing milestone and amazing accomplishment. It really is.

What makes abstinence so significant is that a powerful spiritual dynamic gets flipped; you leave behind a negative cycle of sin management (like being in debt) and move into a cycle that spirals upward. Bogged down in the transactions of sin management, spiritual life revolves around "not sinning" and then when we have sinned, "not feeling guilty." That's not an exciting adventure. But crossing that threshold, spiritual life is experienced positively in the form of growing and loving and doing and sharing. Growing in love is a wonderful thing, freed from the introspection of guilt and sin-management and free to move out with Jesus into the lives of others.

Don't get me wrong, the Christian life will always be a war, but there are better battles. There are battles to take new ground or rescue others instead of taking and retaking the same piece of ground, over and over again.

Abstinence from masturbation yields another dynamic. Habits are momentum. The rut of negative momentum is perpetuated by thoughts like, "I screwed up yesterday, why not today?" When you have a track record of purity there is momentum and motivation to sustain it. Each day, each decision builds a wall, creates distance, and makes the thought of going back more unthinkable.

So this is where we want to be, this is where we're headed. Let me close with a few practical things I've heard or learned along the way.

1. **Debauchery is one of those biblical words you come across that you don't really know the meaning of, but you kinda sorta do.**
   To be specific, it means excessive living: over-eating, over-drinking, and over-sleeping. It's the dynamic that occurs when excess in one area of life (or sloth) overflows to others. I mean, you assume that a person who sleeps and plays video games all day doesn't have a good track record with masturbation. Such are the physics of laziness and debauchery.

2. **Keep your room clean, your bed clean, and your computer clean.**
   We are body and soul, and physical cleanliness affects purity.

3. **Don't play with yourself and don't hang around naked (get dressed right away after a shower).**
   God, I sound like your mother. It is simply a truism that either of these things lead toward masturbation, as do long showers.

4. **Keep the door of your room open all the time.**
   You can remember with the easy acronym KTDOYROATT. Stay away from the Internet late at night. Or SAFTILAN.

Grow in purity, my friend, and move toward the righteousness and freedom of Kingdom living. Don't be discouraged by set-backs, just keep going. Move toward abstinence with masturbation. It will be a significant point on the journey and an enormous weight lifted from your life.

### Reflection

I can't think of any questions that wouldn't feel ridiculous to ask and humiliating to answer. So let's pretend we've reflected and move on, agreed?

# THIS FAR AND NO FURTHER

## WITHIN THE SAFETY OF BORDERS

Well, here is something quite unexpected: there's a lot of kissing going on in the New Testament. I mean, nothing gross, sloppy, sexy, or sensual, but a lot of kissing all the same:

> Greet one another with a holy kiss. All the churches of Christ send greetings.
> Romans 16:16

> All the brothers here send you greetings. Greet one another with a holy kiss.
> 1 Corinthians 16:20

> Greet all the brothers with a holy kiss.
> 1 Thessalonians 5:26

That wouldn't be such a bad standard to have in a dating relationship: nothing gross, sloppy, sexy, or sensual. It could become the new acronym in Christian dating: "Frank, we should probably put an end to the rule of NGSSS." Speaking of dating boundaries, blogger John Crist writes, "you know your physical boundaries in dating relationships have gone too far when..."

- Your boundaries include the phrase "only once a month." If you have a clause that states 'If we follow these rules faithfully for a month we get to reward ourselves by engaging in 30 minutes of premarital spooning once per month"... then your boundaries/motives for actually having boundaries probably need to be reevaluated.

- Your boundaries include the words "but only when we're standing up." Anything that you can do laying down, you can probably do standing up. And now it's going to look REALLY awkward when your roommate accidentally walks in on you. Casually stating, "We were just trying be faithful to our boundaries," isn't going to ease the awkwardness.

- There are adjectives involved. We can kiss, but just no "aggressive" kissing. Or my personal favorite, we can kiss, but not for "extended" periods of time. Good luck defining those adjectives when you're in the moment.

That's certainly funny, and boundaries can be a little ridiculous, but they come from a good place if it's a desire to honor God and "make no provision for the flesh, to gratify its desires" (Romans 13:14). Getting back to New Testament kissing: I think there's something applicable here to dating relationships and the question, "How far is far enough?"

### Holy Kiss

As infants, as children, as adults, physical contact is the primary way we show care, protection, affirmation, and love for one another. I mean, how would you know you played a good game if the coach didn't smack you on the fanny?

Think for a moment of the different ways physical contact expressed care to you when you were growing up. Here's one of mine. I grew up outside New York City and in the 70's and 80's, before Giuliani cleaned it up, the city was an absolute cesspool, particularly Times Square. When I went into the city with my father, walking the streets of midtown, he would have his hand on the small of my back. When I think about it, the message to strangers was, "don't come near him." To me it said, "I love you, you have nothing to fear, I'm protecting you."

This is what interests me in the idea of a "holy kiss." It's the principle of intimate physical contact — which we all need to express and receive — that isn't sexual in nature. In the context of dating this could be any number of expressions of physical closeness without a motive of sexual arousal. With the concept of "holy affection" in mind, I think decisions of what's appropriate become intuitive. And an intuitive guide is what you want because mapping and specifying particulars, as John Crist humorously pointed out, gets a little ridiculous.

## WHAT DOES IT MEAN

Implicit in this idea of holy kiss is a physical display of one's feelings and affections and with that a display of the very nature of the relationship. Physical tokens "mean" or "symbolize" something. An arm draped over a shoulder — depending on the context — can communicate protective care or oneness or even a degree of possession or ownership.

What sexual intimacy symbolizes, biblically speaking, is the relationship between Christ and his bride, the church. No other human relationship (friends, brothers, sisters, parents) other than a husband and wife reflects this. This is an important reason why sexual stimulation is inappropriate for a non-marital relationship. Physically craving someone who isn't or won't be your spouse symbolizes... well, nothing good.

Physical tokens mean something to one person, but to another person they may mean something different. I watched the interaction of two Christians just before walking into a social event. She was tucking the front of the guy's shirt into the front of his pants. So there are a few options: one, she knows this is a turn-on and she doesn't care; two, this guy isn't turned on and, well, that raises other questions; three, she doesn't realize it's a turn-on and he ought to tell her; or four, it was dark and the woman was actually his mother. Physical contact communicates something unless you're intentionally trying to be ambiguous, and that's not a nice game to play.

Again, I just want to come back to that phrase "holy kiss." It's two words and not a list of rules. It's a big idea, and big ideas inform a thousand little decisions. Appropriate demonstrations of physical affection are intuitive if you're clear on what you want to communicate and what you don't. I'm sure, for example, as a male, you know the exact PPI of pressure to apply to a pat on another man's rear that leaves no questions as to where you stand. When you know what you want to communicate, you just know.

As the guy in the relationship, it would be good for you to initiate an honest conversation with the person you are dating to clarify where you see the relationship and why you want to keep from sexualizing it. The standard of the "Holy Kiss" is not a standard for "how far can I get," or "how far can I steer away from physical contact," but "what ways can I show physical affection that are appropriate to our level of commitment that will not cause sexual arousal?"

Keep your conscience clear and keep it your friend. When lines are blurry, the conscience is invaluable as a guide and it's generally reliable if it's kept clear and cleansed. I've tried to relate here what I believe is the tenor of scripture on sexual intimacy before marriage. Perhaps you'll come to different conclusions. If you do, make sure you keep your conscience clear in accordance with those standards. God luck and be safe out there.

### Reflection

When you think of a good model of a Christian relationship, who comes to mind?

What is it about their relationship that you would like to emulate?

In the things you share and disclose with women, is there integrity in your verbal intimacy (as well as physical intimacy)?

Is flirting an issue for you? How about crude or course innuendo? Do you lead women on?

From a perspective of godliness, how would you rate your phone communication?

Do you need to redraw any of your boundaries?

# THE TRUTH OF PURITY

## THE ONE THING WE KNOW THAT WILL DEFEAT A LIE

> You belong to your father, the devil, and you want to carry
> out your father's desire. He was a murderer from the begin-
> ning, not holding to the truth, for there is no truth in him.
> When he lies, he speaks his native language, for he is a liar
> and the father of lies.
> John 8:44

Think of all the lies, manipulations, half-truths, and deceptions
you've seen or heard just in the last few weeks: commercials,
movies, television shows, Internet posts, news programs, song
lyrics, classroom lectures, political speeches, conversations with
friends. There are many lies contained in these, external to us, too
vast to quantify. But between us and the world is a buffer of falsehood: distorted perception, wrong beliefs, and sinful thoughts — a
veil of lies through which to see the world of lies. All of this makes
what we confidently refer to as reality anything but.

When you look at an object, the visual input provided by your
eye enters the brain and the information is instantly parceled
out for processing along two separate pathways. One of those
pathways is a shortcut directly to the prefrontal cortex; what
arrives along that particular pathway is an undeveloped image.
What it looks like to your brain is similar to a movie streaming
over dial-up: a lot of unintelligible blobs of color — raw, unpro-
cessed visual data.

The visual information traveling along the second, slower pathway arrives about fifty milliseconds later — which is an eternity

in mental processing. But there is a reason it's late. The information detoured through the visual cortex where it was analyzed before it joined with the other parcel of information in the prefrontal cortex. So we actually see the object twice. The first look provides crude macro data (which comes over the first pathway), while the second look (from the second pathway) provides visual evaluation and interpretation. First we see and then our brain tells us what we saw. Perception is always a double take.

Lust is a way of perceiving imagery. There is nothing intrinsically attractive about human genitals; you can condition sexual arousal into something as inanimate as a shoe. Pornography is nothing more than the digital streaming of 1's and 0's, but this isn't what you see when you look at it. You see a particular interpretation of the world having nothing to do with the world as it is or people as they are. Lust is delusional, a fabricated reality.

What cannot survive in a world of lies is truth. And if truth is to remain, the world around it must crumble. In this chapter we want to give attention to truth. Biblically speaking, truth comes in two sizes: truth with a small "t" and truth with a capital "T." Capital T truth is the person of Jesus and truth of God's Word. It's a capital T because it's a personal noun, and it's a personal noun because God is a person. Small t truth is truth in the general sense: the opposite of falsehood or duplicity in our thoughts, actions, and speech. Both truths play a role in the life of purity; why don't we start with the smaller of the t's?

### A Lifestyle of Truth

When we come across the word "truth" in Scripture, we are somewhat conditioned to see the word "scripture" because that's usually the reference. But not always. Look, for example, at Ephesians 6:14:

> Stand firm then, with the belt of truth buckled around your waist, with the breastplate of righteousness in place...

You'd assume that the belt of truth referred to here is Scripture, but not so fast. Throughout his letter to the Ephesians, Paul has a lot to say about truth in the general sense, like when he instructs them to "put off falsehood and speak truthfully" (Ephesians 4:25). In the context of the letter, the belt of truth probably refers to a lifestyle of truthfulness and the protection that such a lifestyle provides in the fray of spiritual battle.

A good word, albeit overused, to describe a truthful way of life is "transparency," or as a friend of mine likes to say, "living with the roof off and walls down." It's sort of ironic, but people claiming to be transparent almost never are. In his book *The Most Personal Addiction*, Joe Zychick defines a lifestyle of honesty and transparency as:

> the attempt to make accurate identifications and communicate them to others. In other words, it's the intention to figure out what's going on and sincerely trying to tell other people what you are aware of. Honesty is the heartbeat of mental health because the mind longs to know and experience itself, and allows the people you value to know you.

What I would add to that definition of truthfulness is the importance of making the same intentional effort to be honest with ourselves and God.

Another characteristic of small "t" truth is "carefulness" or "accuracy" in the words one uses, always guarding against exaggerating or manipulating the truth. I have become increasingly aware how pathologically I manipulate time: when I plan to be home, when I actually got up, what time I'll meet you. At the heart of my incessant manipulation of time is ... I have no idea, but it can't be good. Maybe I was left at a birthday party as a child? Maybe in my heart I'm still metaphorically waiting for a ride home? Okay, good talk.

I think what you find in living life truthfully and transparently is that you're increasingly repelled by the lying, deception and concealment required by sexual sin. Duplicity becomes scandalous to the heart and mind.

Exemplifying Scripture's power (truth with a capital T) we typically think of Jesus jousting against Satan in the wildnerness: "It is written, man shall not live by bread alone..." Matthew 4:4). But look at how Jesus responds to temptation in this other situation:

> He then began to teach them that the Son of Man must suffer many things and be rejected by the elders, chief priests and teachers of the law, and that he must be killed and after three days, rise again. He spoke plainly about this, and Peter took him aside and began to rebuke him. But when Jesus turned and looked at his disciples, he rebuked Peter, "Get behind me, Satan."
> Mark 8:31-33a

Jesus responds here not with capital *T* truth but with little *t* truth. He blurts out, with shocking bluntness, "Peter, Satan is using you as a puppet." That was the truth of the situation and calling it out had resisting power for Jesus. He used that truth as a shield.

So what if, when lies of a lustful nature start flittering about your thoughts, you respond to them with truth? You could, for example, be exceedingly transparent and descriptive in your prayers to God: "Lord, I was just thinking that it wouldn't matter if I quickly went to a website right now." Or, you could text a friend with similar bluntness: "I'm already beginning to get excited about being alone tonight and how I might have opportunity to satisfy my flesh — can you pray and ask me tomorrow how I did?"

I don't know, but in seeing Jesus' response to temptation, I'm thinking there may even be something to voicing the truth out loud — hearing your own voice, and Satan hearing it too. But enough conjecture. What it is for sure is a course toward greater and greater truth in your life and speech and prayers, an ever widening umbrella of protection against the lies of lust.

### The Truth of Scripture

I have not put the truth of Scripture second because it's secondary, but because the first thought is less obvious. I didn't want you to miss it. Scripture is not only truth, but it has the power to renew our minds, strengthen our faith, and inflame our hearts with loving God. Joshua Harris writes:

> Scripture cuts through the confusion and hazy half-truths that our sin generates. It reveals our wrong desires. It rebukes our apathy. It corrects our selfish human thinking. It unmasks the deception of sin. It points us to God's goodness and faithfulness when we're tempted to forget. It counters the false promises of lust with God's true promises...

A component of sin is a perceived dissatisfaction with God. Lust's power comes from the promise that it can provide for our needs and make us happy in a way God cannot. Growing in the truth of Scripture and knowledge of God's word has the effect of mooring our hearts and minds to the better, truer promises of God.

In moments of temptation, our hearts reflexively look to the promises of Scripture as something to cling to and hope in...if there is any in our head to be found. If not, we might respond to ourselves with general truisms (*this is a really, really stupid idea, Rick*), but the problem is that these lack authority. They just don't pack the punch of Scripture, and our hearts can hear the difference.

So by all means, arm yourself with the Word of God. Read it, and think about it, and memorize it. As responses to lust, you might start with the following verses:

> But among you there must not be even a hint of sexual immorality, or of any kind of impurity, or of greed, because these are improper for God's holy people.
> Ephesians 5:3

> Flee from sexual immorality. All other sins a man commits are outside his body, but he who sins sexually sins against his own body. Do you not know that your body is a temple of the Holy Spirit, who is in you, whom you have received from God? You are not your own; you were bought at a price. Therefore, honor God with your body.
> 1 Corinthians 6:18

It is God's will that you should be sanctified: that you should avoid sexual immorality; that each of you should learn to control his own body in a way that is holy and honorable, not in passionate lust like the heathen, who do not know God; and that in this matter no one should wrong his brother or take advantage of him.
1 Thessalonians 4:3-6

I made a covenant with my eyes not to look lustfully at a girl.
Job 31:1

As you memorize, pray them back to the Lord and meditate on them. Allow them to leach through the landfill of thoughts and seep deeply into your heart and mind. I haven't always been successful with Scripture memory, but I've tried something recently that's really helped. I'm trying to memorize a whole book of the Bible (Colossians) because how cool would that be to have a whole book of the Bible in my brain — neural pathways cleaved by Scripture? Because it's something of a project, I'm always working on it and that's a good thing. I hope to move on to memorize 1 Peter next; I'll write another book and let you know how it went.

### Reflection

Is there an area in your life or an issue about which you are less than truthful?

When you're dishonest with others, what does it tend to be about?

How are you getting the truth of Scripture off the page and into your heart?

What are the lies you are prone to believe about yourself?

# WHAT IS IT WORTH TO YOU?

---

## INTRINSIC OR EXTRINSIC — WE ARE MOTIVATED BY REWARD

Having never learned to type, I need to hunt for every key, and that makes writing a book grueling to say the least. To keep myself going, every hour or so — like a fish tossed to a performing seal — I reward myself with a refresh of coffee. The fact that it's only coffee is a good indicator of my writing ability. If I were a great writer like Hemingway, I'd be celebrating each completed paragraph with a shot of whiskey. Urban legend has it that Jack Kerouac wrote *On the Road* in twenty amphetamine-filled days, feeding telegraph paper into a typewriter until he produced a single-spaced, 167-foot long manuscript. I'll just have Folgers.

I'm pondering the idea of "reward," which is what made me think of all this, and the little and not-so-little ways rewards motivate us. I think it's fair to say that for any difficult, prolonged, or grueling task, the motivation of reward is significant. In the face of adversity there has to be some compelling reason to keep going. This is certainly the case spiritually, which is why Scripture is filled with promises of both temporal and future reward. Just to take two examples, look at what Jesus says to the enduring saints in the book of Revelation:

> Be faithful unto death, and I will give you the crown of life. He who has an ear, let him hear what the Spirit says to the churches.
> Revelation 2:10-11

> To the one who conquers I will give some of the hidden manna, and I will give him a white stone, with a new name

written on the stone that no one knows except the one who receives it.
Revelation 2:17

C.S. Lewis wrote: "If we consider the unblushing promises of reward and the staggering nature of the rewards promised in the gospels, it would seem that our Lord finds our desires, not too strong, but too weak." What I think he means is that our problem isn't *selfish* desire but a *lesser* desire that's easily satisfied by a lesser reward.

In this chapter we want to ask and answer the question "Why should we strive for sexual purity?" It's not a hypothetical or rhetorical question: our flesh needs an answer and it's got to be a good one. That answer is that the reward for standing firm against lust is greater than the reward for caving in. While that's the answer, it remains to be seen or demonstrated. That demonstration will be the crux of this chapter. We will look at the biblical promises and rewards held forth for obedience. Biblical rewards come in two varieties: temporal (that which blesses and benefits us now) and eternal. We'll look first at the temporal.

### Temporal Rewards

1 Thessalonians 4:6 states, "that in this matter [the matter of sexual immorality] no one should wrong his brother or take advantage of [literally, "steal from"] him." This is a peculiar angle by which to see sexual immorality, viewing it as property theft. But it's not a strange idea for those who are married and have had to deal with thoughts and images of their partner with someone else. It's not a strange idea for those who have showed up on their honeymoon without purity to either give to or receive from their spouse. In fact, it's not a strange idea at all: in such circumstances it's very clear that someone took something that didn't belong to them.

The alternative to this is the reward of faithfulness by bringing your entire self to the marriage and *not* bringing a whole lot of baggage. Uncompromised devotion and purity is a precious thing to give to your spouse and to receive from them. This is a reward worth striving for — a gift to give, a gift to get. Who wants to wake up Christmas morning to gifts already opened — worn, damaged and played with by someone else?

### Spiritual Vitality

In high school we had a rather unkind label for kids who smoked too much pot. We called them Burnouts. Some of them had been great athletes and bright students, but a side effect of cannabis is a generalized loss of vitality, at least for life in the real world. They had no inertia, no drive to engage, change, and influence the real world. Why was that?

Everyone longs for a better life, that's universal. And that longing and discontent triggers engagement with the world. There is a desire to compete, create, change, knock-down, rebuild, protest, or whatever else is required to bend reality to our ideal. It takes drive to make a nest out of the thorns of a fallen world.

Those burnouts, however, found their utopia in a mental state, and the result was passivity and disengagement from the world as it really is. They were ghosts. Pornography is its own utopia and sustained use is similarly pacifying, blunting creativity, confidence, passion, and initiative. Pornography turns men into boys, incapable of eye contact with other adults. But the reward of sexual purity is spiritual and emotional strength and confidence, mental and creative vitality, and the drive necessary to live a godly life and make an impact on a godless world.

### Intimacy

The struggle against pornography and lust can monopolize our devotional life, crowding out intimacy with the logistic transactions of sin management. It's like a married couple who spend all their time worrying and arguing over finances rather than enjoying each other.

There are so many other ways to grow in Christ, and so much more to know about him if we can just get out of the ghetto of sin management. The reward of any relationship is greater intimacy. "It is this potential for intimacy," John Piper writes, "that doesn't just make us pursue purity, but prefer it."

So the reward that is before us is an intimacy with Christ greater than we're experiencing if we're stuck in the rut of sexual defeat. As it says in Hebrews 6:1:

> Therefore, let us leave the elementary teachings about Christ and go on to maturity, not laying again the foundation of repentance from acts that lead to death, and of faith in God.

### Eternal Rewards

Iron, magnesium, hydrogen, helium . . . if you ever gave thought to where those ninety-two elements on the Periodic Table came from, you would probably assume, as most scientists did, that they were simply part of the universe from its beginning. In fact, no one thought any differently until 1957, when the famous astrophysicist Fredrick Hoyle published a paper on stellar nuclear synthesis, or in less technical terms, "how a galactic star burns itself down to nothing."

Hoyle proposed that only two elements, hydrogen and helium, existed at the beginning of the universe, and these two elements coalesced into stars. Extreme gravity inside the star causes the hydrogen to fuse with helium and this process is what "lights" the star and turns it into a massive fireball.

Eventually, after a couple billion years, a star burns through its fuel supply of hydrogen and helium, and as it does so, it produces the next few elements on the Periodic Table: lithium, boron, beryllium, and carbon. This brings us to six elements in the universe.

But the star, like some crazed pyro intent on incinerating itself, proceeds to burn through those elements and creates six more in the process, all the way up to magnesium on the Periodic Table. But these too must go — everything must burn. In fact, as the star burns itself down, it creates the first twenty-six elements of the Periodic Table, all the way to iron. But that's where the fire dies, "Iron is the final peal of a star's natural life."

So where do the rest of the elements in the universe — elements twenty-seven through ninety-two (cobalt through uranium) — come from? Well, when a star finally burns itself down to a cold iron core, it dies. But, oh, what a death, described by Sam Kean in his book *The Disappearing Spoon*:

> Suddenly lacking the energy to keep their full volume, burned out stars implode under their own immense gravity, collapsing thousands of miles in just seconds. Then, rebounding from this collapse, they explode outward. For one glorious month, a supernova stretches millions of miles and shines brighter than a billion stars. During a supernova so many gazillions of particles with so much momentum collide so many times per second that they high jump over the normal energy barriers. Every natural combination of element and isotope spews forth from this particle blizzard.

So here is the awaited analogy — and thank you for your patience. In the worldly furnace of trials and temptation, certain *elements* of godliness are produced in our lives: patience, kindness, self-control, etc. Such *elements* could only be forged in the crucible of earthly sanctification. But when Christ appears, sanctification will be subsumed in a glorious supernova of resurrection power, "taking our weak mortal bodies and transforming them into glorious bodies like [Christ's]" (Philippians 3:21); "we will all be changed — in a flash" (1 Corinthians 15:51–52); and we shall "shine like the brightness of the heavens" (Daniel 12:3) with a whole new array of elemental gifts and capacities.

The doctrine of rewards would lead us to understand that at the moment of our transformation, what we are formed into will have everything to do with what we are formed from (1 Corinthians 15). The raw material of that supernova will be us: our choices, thoughts, actions, attitudes, character, our entire life, and what has been made of it. Our unique, individual life will be magnified, glorified, and transformed. Our reward will be the resulting likeness in our radiance, however bright; in our capacities, however gifted; in our being, however glorious; in our magnitude, however attractive. Our reward will not simply be upon us; it will be us.

Unfairly, it would seem, talent, beauty, intellect, education, wealth, and opportunity are meted out in this world without regard to personal merit. Brad Pitt does not deserve to look like Brad Pitt, he deserves to look like... me. Rewards flip this right-side up. Our life *here* determines what will be innate to us there.*

Concerned that the grueling nature of perseverance in the face of opposition will send his church members seeking comfort and release in old habits of sin, the apostle Peter says:

> Therefore, prepare your minds for action; be self-controlled; set your hope fully on the grace to be given you when Jesus Christ is revealed. As obedient children, do not conform to the evil desires you had when you lived in ignorance.
> 1 Peter 1:13-14

Someday we will be very glad we struggled as we did, fought as we did, and persevered as we did for our purity. It truly will be worth it — worth it forever.

### Ready To Go

Do you know what I've always found compelling? The apostle Paul could look at his Christian life and feel that he was ready to receive his reward then.

> Now, there is in store for me the crown of righteousness, which the Lord, the righteous Judge, will award to me on that day — and not only to me, but also to all who have longed for his appearing.
> 2 Timothy 4:8

One of the things about struggling with lust and pornography is that you don't feel ready to be with Jesus. It feels as though

**91**

there's still unfinished business, like leaving Goliath still standing — still mocking — on the battlefield. When we are living and walking in purity, there is an unregretful readiness to see Jesus face-to-face.

### Something to Give

The twenty-four elders fall down before him who sits on the throne, and worship him who lives forever and ever. They lay their crowns before the throne.
Revelation 4:10

I don't know exactly what our rewards will be in heaven. But, from this verse, I can tell it will be something of immense value. I can also tell something else. I can tell why I'll want it and why I'll want it to be of the greatest possible worth. The irreplaceable value of the elders' crowns is not in its wearing but its worshipping. Our reward, like these crowns, will be a means, a vehicle for worshipping and glorifying God. Their purpose and worth make them the commodity of heaven, but here is where they're earned.

What would be the most precious thing you could present to Jesus? I bet it would be your purity, and the reason is the enormous struggle that it's been. To lay before Jesus a crown of purity would be to give him everything because it cost everything: every ounce of perseverance, every ounce of faith, prayer, worship — everything. To be able to put that at Jesus' feet, that would really be something.

* The analogy of the super nova is taken from a recent book I wrote called, *"Up All Night"*.

### Reflection

In this short article I've touched on only a few of the rewards for a life of purity. What are some others?

Because we're all different, not all rewards are equally motivating. Write out specifically what makes the struggle for holiness "worth it" to you.

An intrinsic reward is the reward subsumed in the activity's fulfillment. The reward of battle, for example, is victory. Is there an intrinsic reward to a life of purity? If so, what would that be?

# THE LOST VIRTUE

## COURAGE IS ITS OWN THiNG

Courage isn't typically a topic of conversation. I mean, maybe at West Point it is, but not in civilian life. Why is that? Maybe it's the result of being snubbed as a fruit of the Spirit: there's love, joy, peace, patience, kindness, goodness, gentleness, self-control and... that's it, no courage. When problems arise in our spiritual lives, we look only to the traditional gauges of community, Scripture reading, prayer, fasting, unconfessed sin, et cetera. We don't have a mental warning light that says, "Coward. Running low on courage." And if our problem were cowardice, would we have the courage to admit it? "Yes, sir, I'm a coward, all right. Can't run away from danger fast enough."

Senator John McCain wrote the following in an article entitled "Why Courage Matters":

> Courage is like a muscle. The more we exercise it, the stronger it gets. I sometimes worry that our collective courage is growing weaker from disuse. We don't demand it from our leaders, and our leaders don't demand it from us. The courage deficit is both our problem and our fault. As a result, too many leaders in the public and private sectors lack the courage necessary to honor their obligations to others and to uphold the essential values of leadership. Often, they display a startling lack of accountability for their mistakes and a desire to put their own self-interest above the common good. Corporate America has taken significant blows to its reputation, because too many executives don't have the courage to stand up for what they know is right.

Courage, it would seem, has left the building, and we must go after it before it runs and hides. Being, as it is, so removed from our thinking, we are going to need to bake a theology of courage from scratch. Let's begin at the beginning, with a definition — what is courage?

## What is Courage?

In his book *Orthodoxy*, G. K. Chesterton describes his rather meandering, or perhaps loafing, route to faith. Though Chesterton described it as a "slovenly autobiography," it's a rather unique intellectual journey. For Chesterton, the virtue of courage was a signpost leading to God and away from atheism because it seemed to defy any kind of "survival of the fittest" mentality. This was also the case on September 11 when firemen willingly traded in their lives for strangers unable to save themselves.

For Chesterton, true paradoxes are clearly the fingerprint of a Creator, and Jesus as the God-man was chief among them. In his well-known description of courage in *"Orthodoxy"*, Chesterton beautifully articulates the paradox of courage:

> Courage is almost a contradiction in terms. It means a strong desire to live taking the form of a readiness to die.
> "He that will lose his life, the same shall save it," is not a piece of mysticism for saints and heroes. It is a piece of everyday advice for sailors or mountaineers. It might be printed in an Alpine guide or a drill book. This paradox is the whole principle of courage; even quite earthly or quite brutal courage. A man cut off by the sea may save his life if he will risk it on the precipice. He can only get away from death by continually stepping within an inch of it. A soldier surrounded by enemies, if he is to cut his way out, needs to combine a strong desire for living with a strange carelessness about dying. He must not merely cling to life, for then he will be a coward, and will not escape. He must not merely wait for death, for then he will be a suicide, and will not escape. He

must seek life in a spirit of furious indifference to it; he must desire life like water and yet drink death like wine.

Courage, roughly defined, is a passion for life manifested in a willingness to die; a desire for life that's so strong that one is willing to walk within an inch of death to get it. One must desire "life like water" yet "drinking death like wine."

Let's look at a few biblical examples…

### Biblical Examples

In the Book of Joshua, issued no less than four times in the first chapter, is the following directive: "Be strong and courageous" (Josh. 1:6), "Be strong and very courageous" (1:7), "Be strong and courageous"(1:9), "Only be strong and courageous" (1:18). God, being omniscient, can see the future. So what are we to conclude from this repetitive charge, except that as God looks forward to the impending battle, there is only one way he foresees that the plan could be in jeopardy and that is if Joshua is a coward.

Here at the most crucial moment in the most crucial battle for the Promised Land, the panoramic view of Scripture narrows to a squint at one person and one virtue. It's as if God says to Joshua, "Everything is going according to plan, and the only way this won't succeed is if you don't have the courage to pull the trigger." Now I'm sure God would have found a way; I'm not endeavoring here to reconcile the sovereignty of God and the cowardice of man. I'm just trying to make a point. There are times in Scripture and times in salvation history when courage is unequivocally what counts.

What is the greatest act of courage in the Bible?

I wonder if you thought immediately of the cross. Surely Jesus' death for our sin is the most courageous act in all of history. What is courage but the willingness to die so that others may live? Jesus died an infinite death to give us an eternal life and this was an act of infinite courage! Yet when we look at the cross, what we often see is an act of love. Having labeled it as such, we rarely see Jesus' courage. Many times, courage is simply not in our field of vision.

Esther, Rahab, Nehemiah, Moses, Daniel, David, Elijah, Paul, Peter, Jeremiah are all models of faith, but they are also models of courage. They all stared down the barrel of a loaded tyrant as Esther did and walked away under their own power. If we remove the faith/faithfulness blinders as we read the Scriptures, courage clearly emerges as a predominant virtue integral to most great acts of faith and redemption.

My point is, Scripture is filled with accounts of unimaginable bravery even when the text doesn't specifically label it as such. And instead of assuming the Holy Spirit blunted all fear and trepidation like morphine, thus making courage superfluous, we should assume that the situations in which the disciples found themselves were every bit as terrifying as they appear and their choice to be obedient was a courageous one, neither easy nor euphoric.

### An Interesting Parallel

In this last biblical example of courage — this one from the New Testament — I want you to see an interesting parallel between it and the Joshua account. More on that in a moment. Chapter 9 is a critical turning point in Luke's gospel, specifically verse 51:

> As the time approached for him to be taken up to heaven, Jesus resolutely set out for Jerusalem.

From this point forward in Luke, we read Jesus' words and actions in the context of His final journey to Jerusalem, in the cast shadow of the cross that awaits Him. All of the events and messages from chapters 10 through 20 are injected with the urgency of catching a departing flight — last warnings, last instructions, last appeals.

One of those last messages is addressed to His disciples. In Luke 12, Jesus is more than just a little concerned about how His disciples will hold up against hostile opposition after He's gone. When the persecution starts, will they be men or mice? The message won't travel far if the messengers won't come out from under the bed.

> I tell you, my friends, do not fear those who kill the body, and after that have nothing more that they can do. But I will warn you whom to fear: fear him who, after he has killed, has authority to cast into hell. Yes, I tell you, fear him! Are not five sparrows sold for two pennies? And not one of them is forgotten before God. Why, even the hairs of your head are all numbered. Fear not; you are of more value than many sparrows.
>
> And I tell you, everyone who acknowledges me before men, the Son of Man also will acknowledge before the angels of God, but the one who denies me before men will be denied before the angels of God...And when they bring you before the synagogues and the rulers and the authorities, do not be anxious about how you should defend yourself or what you should say, for the Holy Spirit will teach you in that very hour what you ought to say."
> Luke 12:4–12

Like the taking of the Promised Land in Joshua, we are at another critical juncture in the plan of redemption — *the* critical juncture. Everything is on the line, literally everything: mankind, the heavens, the earth, the universe, black holes, dark matter, Supernovas... everything. In the impending cosmic battle of the cross and the resurrection, any number of things could threaten the plan. However, as in the book of Joshua, Jesus sees cowardice as perhaps the most menacing. Yes, sir, everything is moving like clockwork: the Son of Man is heading to Jerusalem and there He'll suffer and die. Everything looks to be coming off without a hitch unless ... well, unless His disciples lack the courage to be His witnesses. This would be highly problematic.

And so with words akin to those God spoke to Joshua ("I will never leave you nor forsake you," Joshua 1:5), Jesus assures them that God's presence will go with them: "Don't be afraid; you are worth more than many sparrows," and "Do not worry about how you will defend yourselves or what you will say, for the Holy Spirit will teach you at that time what you should say."

While Jesus' words are encouraging, they are also unyielding.

There is a stern exhortation that retreat or cowardice will be unacceptable. To remove retreat as an option is to restore clarity and focus to a mind fractured with anxiety and fear. Retreat cannot be an option or it will be selected.

Looking at both Joshua 1 and Luke 12, one question is frustratingly unanswered: How? How exactly are we supposed to "be courageous"? What steps do we follow? Typically virtues and vices can be broken down into constituent parts, bite-size pieces that allow us to see the building blocks of love, the steps to forgiveness, or the anatomy of a lie. Courage seems to be a singular, naked act of the will with no stutter steps or stepping stones; you simply choose to act, jump, fight, or throw yourself on a live hand grenade.

I imagine the creative team at Nike arriving at this realization: "Okay, so what moves a person to push themselves, pressing their bodies and minds beyond physical limits, enduring agony and the prospect of failure, humiliation, and defeat?"

"I don't know. They just do it."

## Courage and Purity

C. S. Lewis once wrote, "Courage is not simply one of the virtues, but the form of every virtue at the testing point." In other words, what good is a virtue like honesty if in dire circumstances we'd lie to save our own neck? Without courage we'll shed any virtue at the moment we need it most.

I began this article with the observation that nobody thinks about courage in relation to their spiritual lives. We just don't. But there are critical junctures in the battle against lust where courageous actions and decisions are required. How could they not be required? Conversely, giving up the struggle and surrendering to lust isn't merely failure, but cowardice. We may never label it as such, but that's what it will be — running, hiding from the fight.

So my dear brothers, be strong and be courageous.

### Reflection

Looking at Scripture through the lens of courage, what stands out? Who impresses you?

What is the most courageous thing you've ever done?

What, in your spiritual life, requires courage right now?

Who, for you, serves as a Christian example/model of courage?

Imagine if you were unable to feel fear of anything or anyone: what would you do that you are not doing now?

* Some content taken from *A Million Ways to Die* (Rick James, Cook, 2010)

# YOU'RE FULL OF SOMETHING

**EXPERIENCING THE REALITY OF GOD'S INDWELLING SPIRIT**

> **Valdez Watchstander:** I've got the Exxon Valdez hard
> aground Bligh Reef.
> **Coastguard:** Are you serious?
> **Watchstander:** I'm serious as a heart attack.

At just past midnight on March 24, 1989, while sailing over the
sharp reefs off Bligh Island, the voluminous oil tanker known
as the Exxon Valdez popped like a balloon, deflating 1,264,155
gallons of thick, black, Alaskan Crude into Prince William Sound.
The damage took more than three years and two billion dollars
to clean up, and the toll on Alaska's wildlife was apocalyptic.
Numbered among the casualties: 2,800 sea otters, 250 bald
eagles, 250,000 birds, and 22 killer whales.

The ship's captain, Joseph Hazelwood, had twenty-one years
of experience, an IQ of 132, and had been awake and alert in the
ship's wheelhouse, as several crewmen later testified. While there
were a million unanswered questions, one point was clear from
the investigation: the source of the shipwreck was floating in
Hazelwood's bloodstream, not the Prince William Sound. The
captain admitted to drinking three glasses of vodka before the
Valdez left dock. Still, had the Coast Guard warned the Valdez,
the collision could have been averted, but that wasn't going to
happen because the two men on duty that night both tested positive for alcohol and marijuana. What sunk the Valdez was not a
lack of attention, but a lack of perception.

In his book *Are You Experienced? How Psychedelic
Consciousness Transformed Modern Art*, art critic Ken Johnson

describes what I imagine we already knew about the 60s: cultural perceptions changed radically and drugs played no small part in the revolution. Johnson writes:

> I think psychedelic experience makes you think that there are multiple realities, that there isn't just this one normal real world to which we're supposed to conform, but that the reality changes depending on the state of consciousness that we're in when we're experiencing it.

> It's common to take note of it in pop music... Bob Dylan's music changed in the mid-60s and The Beatles changed, and many of them have publicly acknowledged that they were changed by sampling marijuana and LSD.

> I think the main thing is the idea that in psychedelic experience, people start thinking about their own perceptions. They don't take their perceptions for granted, but they start thinking about how our perceptions work and how interesting it is the way we think about the world.

But with or without drugs, perceptions would have changed in the 60s and that's because ideas, philosophies, politics, media, and culture also influence perception. Alcohol and drugs are just the most obvious, most pained examples of perceptual influence, which is why Paul uses alcohol to talk of perception: "And do not get drunk with wine, for that is debauchery, but be filled with the Spirit" (Ephesians 5:18).

### Guy Walks into a Bar

Interestingly enough, Ephesians 5:18 is not the first time that alcohol and the Holy Spirit are contrasted in the New Testament. In Acts 2, when believers filled with the Spirit are accused of being drunk, the church is faced with a public relations nightmare, which Peter averts by a swift, public rebuttal: "Men of Judea... these people are not drunk, as you suppose" (Acts 2:15).

But whenever two things are contrasted there has to be some baseline of comparison. You wouldn't say, "Never wear a sombrero, but instead be filled with the Spirit"; however, maybe people say this in Mexico all the time, I don't really know. The basis for comparison between alcohol and the Holy Spirit is the idea of influence and how they both affect and alter perception. God's Spirit leads to ever-increasing knowledge of God and apprehension of the truth, and alcohol leads to greater impairment and delusion.

Like a DVD of *Ironing Man* or *Lets Miserable* that sells in Shanghai, alcohol is the cheap knock-off of Spirit-filled transformation, but there are surface similarities between the two. Drunkenness, for example, progresses in degrees, as does the influence of the Spirit. Affection, joy, empathy: inebriation can at least momentarily create such sensations. There is also confidence and courage that comes from the Spirit and we see that in the disciples as they go around boldly proclaiming the gospel. There is a similar loosening of the tongue in someone drunk, as they go around boldly proclaiming... I don't know... songs from the 90's, I guess.

So that all makes sense, but here's what seems odd: the strict either/or choice, as if there were only two possibilities in the world — being drunk or filled with the Spirit. I mean, can't you simply not be under the influence of anything? No, frankly, you can't.

There is no such thing as a "blank slate" (tabula rasa) of perception. Our perception is deluded from the get-go, already distorted through sin, through the flesh, through evil, and through an endless string of other influences (greed, lust, ambition, jealousy, pride, anger, etc.). Deluded is our natural state.

And what this means is being drunk with alcohol is paradigmatic. That is, you could substitute, "do not be drunk with greed" for "do not be drunk with pride." The point is, you're going to be filled with something. No one is sober apart from the regenerating work of the Holy Spirit. You don't get to choose whether your perception is influenced, only what influences it. That's the madness of living in a fallen state, in a fallen world.

## Testing Influence

Sitting in our closet is an enormous box of drug tests. We have a lot of young adults who hang out at our home with addiction issues, so we finally bought in bulk.

The tests are simple enough. Fill the cup and five minutes later you get a color-coded toxicology report. Unfortunately, the Internet now spreads knowledge that once-upon-a-time you could only learn from your cellmate. And so there are websites devoted to mentoring nascent drug users in the chemistry of test manipulation, showing them how to use a drop of Visine or Clorox to get a false negative. It doesn't matter because in the end the most reliable indicator is not the test but the request for a sample. "Dude, I just went" or "Dude, I can't seem to go right now" doesn't bode well; any statement that begins with "Dude" doesn't bode well.

Even still, the drug culture is a world of lies, and tests are indispensable for cutting through the excuses, the denial, and the self-righteous protestations to determine what's really going on. It would be helpful if we could do something similar with our perceptions. Given the stark categories of "being drunk" or "filled with the Spirit," it's natural to assume we're the latter, but I'm not sure that's a good assumption. Maybe we're "drunk" on pride or "filled" with iTunes. How would we know?

## The Salt Water Test

When Jesus spoke of the Holy Spirit's influence within the heart of a believer, he also placed it in contrast, but not with, alcohol:

> Jesus stood up and cried out, "If anyone thirsts, let him come to me and drink. Whoever believes in me, as the Scripture has said, 'Out of his heart will flow rivers of living water. '" By this he meant the Holy Spirit whom those who believed in him were later to receive.
> John 7:37-39

The phrase "living water" sounds mystical, like a location on Tolkien's Map of Middle Earth. But it's not so enchanted. In fact, it was a common designation for "fresh water" in ancient times. The Arabian Peninsula is a seashore of sand and ocean, and that makes fresh water "living water," the only thing that can grow crops, keep animals living, and broadly sustain life. The power of the analogy is that the alternative to "living water" is not dead or stagnant water, it's salt water. And if there's a better metaphor for sin than salt water, I can't imagine what it is.

Salt water is something nearly identical to fresh water except that drinking it makes you thirstier, drinking it actually de-hydrates you. Think about that. Salt water plays the same sick joke that sin plays on us: promising to satisfy our thirst only to increase it. You could float atop an entire ocean of salt water and still die of thirst. Likewise, you could possess the whole world and lose your soul. So where do we go to satisfy our thirst? That's the question, and thirst is the clue.

Throughout the day we experience pangs of thirst and if we aren't conscious of those pangs, and most people aren't, we miss the request our body is making for rehydration. Just watch smokers. Whenever they feel a need (thirst), they light up. If they feel lonely, they light up. If they're nervous, they light up. If they need confidence or motivation, if they're bored or dissatisfied, need clarity or concentration . . . they light up. That's not to single out smokers. Smoking is paradigmatic the way alcohol is paradigmatic: You can do the same thing with music, texting, Facebook, energy drinks, or E*TRADE. The point is, we experience incessant thirst: thirst for comfort, wisdom, strength, encouragement, direction, companionship, stimulation, motivation, etc., and we sip from some canteen all day long.

So there are grotesquely personal questions we need to ask ourselves:

- When you feel the thirst of loneliness, do you turn to the Lord for intimacy? "Lord, I need you; I need to feel connected to you . . ." or do you turn to Netflix or Facebook or pornography to fill the loneliness?

- When you feel the thirst of insecurity do you turn to the Lord and to prayer and to his Word or do you go to the gym, or brag, or put others down, or pretend to be someone you're not? Does insecurity move you to humble dependence or image management? Do you talk to God or is it just self-talk, self-soothing, self-analysis?

- When you feel bored, dissatisfied, or depressed do you fill the vacuum with iTunes, or sleep, or stimulants, or fantasy, or video games, or pornography, or ESPN, or travel, or do you turn to God with your thirst?

All day long we're drinking something and that something is "filling us," and what's filling us is either increasing perception or distorting it. That's the point. To be filled with the Spirit is to be sipping-drawing-drinking-inhaling God's presence to meet those thirsts — a pack a day, maybe more.

We are most susceptible to lust when we are under the influence of something and not fully sober in our judgment. Alcohol can do that but so can staring at football or playing a video game for three hours or having ear buds in or headphones on for hours at a time. These things take us outside ourselves. A day walking in the Spirit is one where you are trying to remain awake and alert to God, constantly connecting with him, mentally grounded, perceptually sober, aware and guarded toward other perceptual influences.

* Some content taken from *Up All Night* (Rick James, NavPress, 2015)

### Reflection

What are those things that have the most influence on your thoughts?

What things put you in a very different mental state?

When do you feel most disconnected from God?

What do you turn to throughout the day, besides God, for energy and empowerment?

How can you put your heart and mind more under the Spirit's influence?

# A CITY NEVER SLEEPS

## Community: The catalyst of Spiritual Wakefulness

Geoffrey West is a theoretical physicist who has devoted his academic life to reducing the vast complexities of the universe to snackable equations. Like Einstein, his interest is in fundamental laws that explain the world around us, and that world is now urbanized. In 2008, the United Nations reported that for the first time in human history, man is "predominantly an urban species." So West set out to find the $E=mc^2$ of an urban metropolis: a simple equation that would describe how and why a city grows.

West compiled every mind-numbing data point from the sum total of electrical wire in Frankfurt to the number of college graduates in Boise. He amassed stats on gas stations and personal income, flu outbreaks and homicides, coffee shops and the walking speed of pedestrians.

After two years of research, what West discovered is that all the roads and buses and crosswalks and skyscrapers and gridlock and everything else that makes a city can be reduced to a few "exquisitely simple equations." Given the population of a city, West can predict, with eighty-five percent accuracy, everything from the average income to the dimensions of its sewer system.

According to West, cities operate at a golden ratio of 1.15. That is, if you moved Jane Smith from a city of 500,000 to a city of one million she would earn 15 percent more money, have 15 percent more restaurants in her neighborhood, possess a 15 percent higher education, file for 15 percent more patents, and be 15 percent more likely to be victimized by violent crimes. "According to the data, whenever a city doubles in size, every measure of economic activity, from construction spending to the amount of bank deposits, increases by approximately 15 percent per capita." Even "pace of life" statistics bear out this 15% scaling: people actually do walk and talk faster in cities.

It may seem normal for the speed of life to be faster in a city, but it's not. Observable, yes; normal, no. Systems of any kind get slower, not faster, as they increase in size. Think of traffic or the slow-moving bureaucracy of government or an overcrowded classroom that stalls to the rate of the slowest learner. Or think about it biologically: the heartbeat of an elephant is way slower than a human's, and a human's is slower than a gerbil's — the rule across nature is that metabolism slows with size. But a city is a system and an organism and yet its metabolism, for some strange reason, gets faster with size.

Of course every rule has exceptions, and that would be a city like Detroit. Detroit functions exactly like traffic or bureaucracy or an overcrowded classroom. For a city to operate at that 1.15 ratio it requires certain things and a healthy sense of community is one of them.

In what is probably the most celebrated study of urban life, *The Death and Life of the Great American City*, Jane Jacobs identified the "mingling of diversity" and the interaction between people of different "social distances" as the difference between a city block and a city neighborhood. Apparently, Detroit doesn't have that and it lacks something else. Like a person tied to a social network, a city is a web of interconnectivity and needs to have pouring into it multiple streams of resources. Detroit had one — automobiles — and when that floundered, so did the city.

In thinking about biblical community, the paradox of cities offers some immediate connections. For one, Scripture affirms the uniqueness of a city if for no other reason than it's a dense population of people made in God's image. Timothy Keller would go a step farther, stating that God uniquely "designed the city with the power to draw out the resources of creation (of the natural order and the human soul) and thus to build civilization." However you see it, you certainly wouldn't want to remove the word Jerusalem from the Bible. I'm not sure what would be left.

But the power of a city is the power of community and Detroit demonstrates that one is not the same as the other. A city without community is the skeleton of a city: structure without animation. And there are certainly churches that are the spiritual equivalent of Detroit. They lack synergy, diversity, interconnectivity, and are wholly dependent on a pastor's dynamism the way Detroit lived and died on the automobile.

And then there's that golden 1.15 ratio, that synergy where the sum is greater than the parts. At some point, whether at a church or a Bible study or a youth group, I'm sure you've experienced it, and when you did, your walk with God was faster.

A life of purity requires the power of community, the accountability of other Christian men, and healthy friendships with godly women. As you think about your spiritual environment, here are some of the influences and resources that you want in your village...

### "Hi, My Name is Rick."

Alcoholics Anonymous (AA) has been one of the few programs that has seen any success in treating alcoholism. The 12 steps of AA are actually built on Christian principles — loosely. Of those who have seen success through the program, most cite Step Five as the turning point. It reads: "Admitted to God, to ourselves and to another human being the exact nature of our wrongs." Confessing to others "the exact nature of wrongs" is why people get well in AA. That is the genius of, "Hello, my name is Bob and I'm an alcoholic."

1 John 1:9 says: "If we confess our sins, he is faithful and just and will forgive us our sins and purify us from all unrighteousness." Notice that the emphasis of confessing to God is on cleansing and forgiveness of our sin. Now look at James 5:16:

> Therefore confess your sins to each other and pray for each other so that you may be healed. The prayer of a righteous man is powerful and effective.

Do you see the difference in emphasis? Confessing to others helps us heal and get better. Admitting our sin, articulating it, seeing grace incarnated in the face of a friend, prioritizing spiritual wellness over image management: all of these things change us and help us get well.

Who in your community would be a good person to share "the exact nature of your wrongs?"

## A Lifting Partner

When you go to the gym, you typically see two guys standing by the bench-press, and that's because one guy on his own will wind up with a barbell wrapped around his neck. Anyone serious about fitness trains with a partner.

I got an unusual call from a friend struggling with lust. What was unusual was he was calling before he lusted, before he looked at pornography, before he went on his computer, before he was alone. He hadn't done anything. Yet he could see the direction of his thoughts and where the day was heading and he stopped it with a call of accountability. An accountable relationship is like that; it's a lifting partner, not a therapist. Anyone serious about holiness trains with a partner.

In a *New Yorker* article entitled "Group Think," Malcolm Gladwell describes the communal lifestyle of the original cast of Saturday Night Live, a relational dynamic responsible for the renaissance of modern comedy. Gladwell writes:

> In the early days of SNL [Saturday Night Live] Everyone knew everyone and everyone was always in everyone else's business, and that fact goes a long way toward explaining the extraordinary chemistry among the show's cast. Belushi would stay overnight at people's apartments, and was notorious for getting hungry in the middle of the night and leaving spaghetti-sauce imprints all over the kitchen... Newman would hang out at Radner's house, and Radner would be eating a gallon of ice cream and Newman would be snorting heroin... "There we were," Newman recalls, "practicing our illnesses together."

I really love that line, "There we were, practicing our

illnesses together." I think that's a good definition of accountable relationships.

## Cyber Community

The internet is a bit like a neighborhood in the process of gentrification. There's a dangerous element out there. Cyber thieves are everywhere, or at least in all the coffee shops of Eastern Europe. Unrestrained by law, conscience, or national allegiance, you would think these criminal savants would have stolen the Internet and everything on it. But that hasn't happened, and it's because the virus of cybercrime stimulated the Web's immune system. An entire industry of net security has arisen to defend us: massive firewalls bar intruders, cyber-cops infiltrate chat rooms, sophisticated software shields networks and mainframes, and White Hats — the unfallen angels of cyberspace — stand watch over unwitting mortals. All of which is to say, if you don't have an internet filter, you should get one. Technology used for ill can also be used for protection.

I use a filter called Covenant Eyes. I'm not a spokesman for them or anything, but I've found it very helpful and effective. Besides the internet filter, you choose someone or several people to receive a weekly log of any websites that were, how should we say...questionable? In turn, your friend or friends should reach out to you if it looks like it's been a rough week. It's helpful. I mean, who in the world wants their friends see that they went to peoplewhostandontheirheadnaked.com? To join the program, go to **covenanteyes.com**. There are other great products out there, as well, to save you from unbridled autonomy.

## Men's Health

For sanity, health, growth, relationships, and humor, you absolutely have to get involved in Guy's Bible study. There really is something about a group of Christian guys at the same stage of life, all pursuing God. This cannot be duplicated in any other venue. Bonds are created that last for years, and these bonds bridge life's difficult patches. In the midst of writing this today, I got an email from a guy I was in Bible study with over twenty years ago. His marriage isn't doing so well and he knows I'm here for him and vise versa.

If you're not part of a group, then start one. Use the material provided in this book as a foundation and then move on to a regular study of Scripture together.

### Cities Never Sleep

A city caught in a cycle of negative momentum is inevitably due to a lack of economic diversity — remember Detroit. Most Christians have only a single lifeline tying them to the body of Christ and when that lifeline is lost due to a move or some falling out, spiritual entropy sets in. Lost is not only the community but the drive to find or create a new one. So let me encourage you to diversify now and create as many communal strands as you can. Build a city.

\* Some content taken from *Up All Night* (Rick James, NavPress, 2015)

### Reflection

When I say "build a spiritual city" around your life, what immediately comes to mind?

What other insights come to mind in viewing your life as a city?

What's missing in your city?

If your spiritual life were to wind up like Detroit, try to project why that would be.

# LIVING TOGETHER

## WHY WE TAKE HOLINESS SERIOUSLY

When we put our faith in Christ, it is the person of the Holy Spirit who enters our lives, fills our hearts, and makes his home with us. God indwells us and that's a really big thought. Some thoughts are just too big to house in your head, like: right now the earth is spinning at over 1,000 mph... what do you do with that?

But there is a reality to God's presence that has to be grasped at some level which is why Paul writes to the Corinthians:

> Flee from sexual immorality. All other sins a man commits are outside his body, but he who sins sexually sins against his own body. Do you not know that your body is a temple of the Holy Spirit, who is in you, whom you have received from God?" You are not your own; you were bought at a price. Therefore honor God with your body.
> 1 Corinthians 6:18-20

In reminding them of God's indwelling, Paul brings to mind a practical — and in this case, tragic — implication. Due to God's presence within us, our lust filled actions and fantasies are played out in the courts of God's holy Temple where he dwells.

To fully grasp the weight of this Temple analogy, we need some historical context and that's what I'd like to give you in this chapter. But let me be clear about the context in which we are talking about this. The point of this study is not for us to feel any worse than we already do about lust, pornography, or past sexual relationships. See, the problem with the Corinthians was they saw nothing wrong with recreational sex, and that's a different problem altogether. They should have felt guilty but they didn't. If you're reading this book then you're neither ambivalent nor rebellious about your lustful failings and that's not you — it's not you at all.

For you, for me, the power of this biblical picture is to protect us, and to keep our hearts and minds safely distant from doing things we don't want to do. In essence, the help provided by internet accountability arrangements is the help provided by knowing someone else is going to see exactly what you looked at. Such knowledge is a hedge of protection, and so is the knowledge of God's indwelling Spirit. So, with that ground work, let's reconstruct the Temple.

### The Beginning of Acts

At the end of the first chapter in the Book of Acts, the disciples are looking to replace Judas, and they put a full team of twelve out on the playing field. They propose two men: Joseph called Barsabbas and Matthias, and then they pray for God's guidance: "Lord, you know everyone's heart. Show us which of these two you have chosen to take over this apostolic ministry." But then the text tells us that "they cast lots" and "the lot fell on Matthias, and he was numbered with the eleven apostles" (Acts 1:26).

Casting lots for direction is a little disturbing, like throwing a witch into a pond to see if she floats kind of disturbing. As a means of discerning God's providence, casting lots wasn't uncommon in the Old Testament. But it seems odd and out of place here in the New Testament, among Jesus' disciples. That oddness? You're supposed to feel that. Casting lots is out of place and the story is situated here to show us why and what changed. For recorded in Acts chapter 2 — immediately following the casting lots — is Pentecost and the coming of the Holy Spirit. From this time forward, the indwelling Spirit will lead God's people, not providence. But we've gotten ahead of ourselves. Put a mental bookmarker in Acts 2, and let's gain a little historical perspective.

## Out of Egypt

It's about 1446 B.C. and as the Israelites exit out of Egypt, they head to Mount Sinai, the chosen place of God's presence before Israel. The reality of God's presence at Sinai was manifested and impressed upon the people by rumblings, smoke, and fire coming from the mountain. At Sinai, God tells Moses that his presence will accompany Israel to the land promised and he gives Moses instructions to build a Tabernacle, a portable tent that will serve as the place of God's presence among Israel as they travel to Canaan.

So they build the tabernacle, following carefully all the details and instructions given them by God. Upon completion of the structure, Israel gathers to pray and dedicate the Tabernacle to the Lord, and the structure is quite literally, and viscerally, filled with his presence, evoking in Israel the same awe and fear they felt at Mount Sinai:

> Then the cloud covered the Tent of Meeting, and the glory of the LORD filled the tabernacle. Moses could not enter the Tent of Meeting because the cloud had settled upon it, and the glory of the LORD filled the tabernacle.

This happened only at the Dedication: a dramatic display of God's presence to reinforce the gravity of keeping the Tabernacle holy and undefiled.

## The Temple

Now, if you were paying attention you'll remember I said that the Tabernacle was like a portable temple or tent. God's dwelling among Israel would remain in this tent for roughly the next 450 years until King David's son, Solomon, builds its permanent re-placement, the Temple in Jerusalem.

So somewhere around 986 B.C., Solomon completes work on the Temple, and the day of Dedication arrives. After Solomon prays and dedicates the Temple we read...

When Solomon finished praying, fire came down from heaven and consumed the burnt offering and the sacrifices, and the glory of the LORD filled the temple. The priests could not enter the temple of the LORD because the glory of the LORD filled it. When all the Israelites saw the fire coming down and the glory of the LORD above the temple, they knelt on the pavement with their faces to the ground, and they worshiped and gave thanks to the LORD, saying, "He is good; his love endures forever."
2 Chronicles 7:1-3

It is literally a repeat of the same phenomenon that occurred at the dedication of the Tabernacle 450 years earlier, rehearsing, once again, in the mind of the people that God dwells in the Temple and every effort must be made to keep it holy. In the centuries that follow, the Temple would be the hub of Israel's social, political, and religious life; it was the heart of Israel and everything circulated to it and from it.

Now here's where the story could get confusing, so pay attention. In about 600 BC (about 380 years after the building of the Temple), Israel is exiled from the land by invading Babylonians. The exile is God's discipline for Israel's disobedience and it has been a long time coming. In the process, Jerusalem is ransacked and Solomon's Temple is demolished.

During exile, prophets affirm God's promise to restore Israel to her land and, sure enough, seventy years later they are back in Israel, and the first thing the returning exiles do is start construction on the Temple.

### The Rebuilt Temple

The rebuilding of the Temple takes about twenty years which bring us to about 520 BC, if you're counting. Unfortunately, due to a shortage of resources, it does not compare to the splendor of Solomon's Temple; it is more like the splendor of a 7-11. Nevertheless, they dedicate their new Temple just as Solomon did, and lo and behold... nothing. No sparks. No smoke. Nothing. This is a disappointment to say the least, but disappointment turns to expectation as the prophets promise a future Temple, more glorious than Solomon's. The builder of this future Temple will be none other than the messiah, and so it was that Israel's messianic hope became intimately tied to the promise of a new Temple.

### The Coming of Christ

Well, as we know, the messiah came and was crucified and res-urrected. The messianic plan does not unfold in a way anyone expected, and there is considerable confusion on the part of the disciples. Knowing certainly that Jesus is the Messiah (this is after the resurrection), they don't understand what's happened to the new Temple, the restoration of Israel, and the pouring out of God's Spirit; they are not seeing the things everyone expected to see with the Messiah's coming. In the first chapter of Acts, just prior Jesus' Ascension, the disciples articulate this very question: "Lord, will you at this time restore the kingdom to Israel?"

The full answer to their question comes in Acts chapter 2:

> When the day of Pentecost came, they were all together in one place. Suddenly a sound like the blowing of a violent wind came from heaven and filled the whole house where they were sitting. They saw what seemed to be tongues of fire that separated and came to rest on each of them. All of them were filled with the Holy Spirit and began to speak in other tongues as the Spirit enabled them.
> Acts 2:1-4

Now, if you're a Jewish Christian — like the disciples — you'd be ecstatic. The anticipation of the powerful coming of the Holy Spirit, throughout the Old Testament, is a hallmark of the Messiah's reign. You would finally be able to tell your neighbors, "Hah! Told you so! Jesus is the Messiah." But you would also still wonder: where is the new Temple the Messiah was going to build? What will house this new outpouring of God's Spirit upon the church?

Then, it dawns on you. *You* are the Temple. God's presence dwells within you. Together with other believers you will comprise a structure occupying the entire world. Crazy.

### What are the Implications of the Holy Spirit Dwelling in Me?

There are countless implications and promises associated with the indwelling of God's Spirit, but we will simply finish where we began this article:

> Flee from sexual immorality. All other sins a man commits are outside his body, but he who sins sexually sins against his own body. Do you not know that your body is a temple of the Holy Spirit, who is in you, whom you have received from God?" You are not your own; you were bought at a price. Therefore honor God with your body.
> 1 Corinthians 6:18-20

An obvious entailment of the Holy Spirit in us, and the focus of Paul's instruction to the Corinthians, is that sexual immorality is done in the presence of the Lord, performed in the Temple itself. Yikes. To a first-century Jew (as the disciples were) the idea of this would have been unutterable. It has little of that effect on us, but I hope the historical context has restored some of its meaning and motivation for you. You are the Temple of the living God.

\* Some of the concepts found in this article are from Gordon Fee's work, *God's Empowering Presence*.

### Reflection

How have you experienced the reality of God's presence in you?

Besides sexual purity, what's another implication of God's presence indwelling you?

With a fresh awareness of his presence, take some time to confess any sin or impurity that comes to mind.

# MAKE UP YOUR MIND

---

## RESOLVED IN A RIGHT WAY

Of all the New Testament passages applicable to lust, few exceed these verses in importance:

> Let not sin therefore reign in your mortal body, to make you obey its passions. Do not present your members to sin as instruments for unrighteousness, but present yourselves to God as those who have been brought from death to life, and your members to God as instruments for righteousness. For sin will have no dominion over you, since you are not under law but under grace.
> Romans 6:12-14

The idea is simple enough. Don't let sin rule your life or govern your thoughts, plans, dreams, feelings, and actions. Insight is lost in the imagery, and imagery is lost in the translation.

The New Testament has what theologian Gordon Fee calls a "symbolic universe" — words that carry with them an imported meaning. That imported meaning comes from the world of the Old Testament. Certain Old Testament analogies are obvious, says Fee, but many words and phrases contain a meaningful echo for those who have grown up with or have been saturated in Old Testament stories.

Fee illustrates what he means by relaying a conversation he once had with an Australian. During the conversation, he threw out the phrase, "four score and seven years ago" to which the Australian responded, "What does 84 years have to do with anything?" That phrase from the Gettysburg Address is a part of the symbolic universe of America and is totally lost on outsiders, or at the very least, Australians. So here's the point: for a first-century Jewish-Christian, Romans 6 would have echoed Joshua's call to Israel to decide, once and for all, who they would serve with their hearts and lives:

> But if serving the LORD seems undesirable to you, then choose for yourselves this day whom you will serve, whether the gods your forefathers served beyond the River, or the gods of the Amorites, in whose land you are living. But as for me and my household, we will serve the LORD.
> Joshua 24:15

In a previous chapter we looked at the history of Israel and what was involved in their taking possession of the Promised Land. Israel vacillated for years in their conquest, leaving large portions of the land unclaimed and unconquered. Finally, speaking for the Lord, Joshua says to Israel, "Enough already. Are you going to rule over your enemy or allow your enemy to rule over you? Make up your mind...now."

Spiritual growth encompasses many overlapping efforts (prayer, Scripture, obedience, etc.), and our will binds these efforts together and marches them toward a goal. So it's a pretty big deal when we decide to commit our will to something or someone. Not much happens until we do. That's what Joshua was calling for. That's what Romans 6 is calling for: a commitment of the will to fight whole heartedly in the battle.

This commitment is not a vow to never stumble, but rather to never turn back (every war has its lost battles). It's a resolve to strive with all of God's resources and strength, and with all of ours, to the highest possible standard of purity. It is a commitment to perseverance and to never give up or give in no matter how many setbacks. And it's a commitment to take whatever action necessary, no matter how drastic, to gain victory.

In this, I want to encourage you to make a definitive choice to fight and not stop fighting until victory has been decisive.

### Afterword

In the movie *The Shawshank Redemption*, Tim Robbins plays Andy Dufresne, a messianic figure wrongly accused of a crime and sentenced to life in prison. If you don't immediately see the symbolism, it becomes clear when Andy's first miracle is to convince the guards to give the prisoners beer, much like Jesus' first miracle of turning water to wine.

The movie builds up to Andy's miraculous escape in which he crawls five hundred pitch-black yards through a rotting, fully operational sewage pipe. It is a powerful — indeed redemptive — scene as Dufresne emerges from the sewer covered in the stink of death into a cleansing rain. He is transformed, washed clean, and purified from human stain. All this while, narrator Morgan Freeman eulogizes, "Andy crawled through a river of s*** and came out clean on the other side."

I'll see you on the other side, dear friend.

# KEEP MOVING

---

## GETTING WELL, WHILE HELPING OTHERS GET WELL

God does some crazy stuff in the Book of Acts, and many believe that the direct and dramatic guidance given by the Holy Spirit is due to the uniqueness of the apostolic age, an age without a New Testament to guide it. But I think the reason is simpler — less theological, anyway. I think the early Christians received special leading and direction from God because they needed it.

These men and women were actively proclaiming the gospel, aggressively pushing the boundaries of Christ's kingdom. This requires real-time intelligence: who to speak to, what to say, how to say it, where to go next. Quite honestly, our days don't require much of that — fries or onion rings, oh Lord? Turn thine eyes to thy hungry servant.

This is something the Christian counseling movement never got right: the need to stay on mission. It is ministry that makes us conduits of the Spirit and protects our hearts from self-absorption. There isn't a lot of biblical support for the idea of pulling away to work on ourselves, focusing on our growth and healing divorced from helping others.

What if the lack of empowerment we experience from the Spirit isn't a sin or prayer or listening problem? What if it's a lack of involvement in the activities that require God to speak, lead, and empower? It's quite possible, you know. The book of Acts is a record of the church on mission. We have no record of first-century believers going about the daily grind but still being moved about like chess pieces. When Jesus spoke of God's will and God's provisions he said "seek first the kingdom of God," and all the other things would be "added."

## A Shared Mission

Last year I was invited to a small Jesuit university in the Midwest to speak evangelistically on the historical Jesus. As it turned out, I hadn't actually been invited, but I didn't know that until I got there.

When I showed up on campus I was met by three of the student leaders from the Christian Fellowship, but not really. There was no Christian Fellowship, no officers, no bylaws, just three guys named Grant, Kyle, and Ryan. These guys had heard me speak at some conference and figured they'd have me come to their campus and "you know, do whatever."

At 7 p.m. we were all sitting in the Student Union, and as far as I knew, I was speaking at a campus-wide event in an hour. But clearly something wasn't right: there was no publicity, no sign of an impending event, and Grant, Kyle, and Ryan were glancing around the Student Center like a heist was in progress. Then Grant, apparently spotting someone, cryptically said to the others, "They know we're going to try to meet tonight."

They finally explained the situation to me. Over the previous month, a drama had unfolded between the young men and the parochial administration. The university's policy was that only an approved Catholic priest could speak on matters of faith, and in light of the wife and children mentioned in my bio, I am clearly not a priest, or at least not a very good one.

And so the administration had expressly forbade my coming to campus: no meeting room, no publicity, no sound system, no invitations, no event, period. But these guys had decided to do it anyway, and so I found myself hunkered down with an underground church of sorts: a handful of passionate believers who met together, prayed together, and purposed together to proclaim the gospel in an environment hostile to such efforts.

Well, in for a dime, in for a dollar, so I asked Grant, "What are we going to do?" Grant said — and as I picture it now he's speaking out of the side of his mouth, but really he wasn't — "There are meeting lounges in the basement of a building on the other side of campus. We'll try there."

"But how are students going to know about the meeting?"

I asked Grant. He said, "We're going to text everyone we know, tell them where and when, and see who shows up." I liked this idea because I didn't have another one.

So we walked across campus, down into the basement of some 70s building which appeared to be forged in the architectural train-wreck of Catholic Modernism when crucifixes were sleeked down to hood ornaments and Jesus took on the appearance of a totem on Easter Island. There in the catacombs of Alfred E. Newman Hall, the boys texted and we waited to see who would come. By eight o'clock, eighty-odd students had packed into the room. Grant was going to give it another ten minutes because people were still trickling in, but Bobby — who had been standing look-out in the hall — rushed in looking panicked and said, "Mrs. Woodrow is coming."

Mrs. Woodrow was the dean of students. She wasn't a nun, but she had the biceps of one. We all peeked out into the hallway and sure enough, the Wicked Witch of the West was clomping down the linoleum runway, not looking pleased, no sir, not pleased at all. So Grant looked at me and said, "Just start. Just start the talk. It will be too awkward for her stop the meeting if you're already talking." I liked this idea because I didn't have another one.

So I hopped up in front of everyone and just began talking. Ten seconds later I could see Mrs. Woodrow outside in the hallway. Grant was right, she wasn't going to interrupt me while I was talking. So I kept talking and didn't stop for an hour. When I did, it was to give the students an opportunity to place their faith in Christ. During the entire talk, Mrs. Woodrow paced outside in the hallway.

When I finally finished and the students started to get up from their seats, Mrs. Woodrow plowed into the room, "Excuse me, excuse me. What is your name and who invited you here?"

"I'm just a friend of Grant, Kyle, and Ryan." That's all I said, and as it turned out, a lawyer couldn't have crafted it better because there are no rules about students having friends visit them on campus. I mean, it's weird they have a fifty year-old friend, but weird isn't against school policy.

Afterward, we went back to one of their rooms to see what students had written on the comment cards:

"No way, April says she wants to hear more about Christ."
"Check this out, Mark says he trusted Christ."
"He did not!"
"Read it yourself."

It went on and on like that, and I sat there listening, experiencing the Christian church as it was in the beginning, as it's come down to us today, and as it still is in many parts of the world. I experienced the church as a missional community.

By missional, I mean Grant, Kyle, and Ryan were actively engaged in expanding Christ's kingdom through the preaching of the gospel. In the cosmic struggle, no good deed goes unpunished, so they were experiencing persecution in response to their evangelistic efforts. These are two powerful ingredients and when mixed together create the thick, rich broth of community. Mission unites believers in vision and purpose while persecution huddles the community for safety and strength, and the combination brings prayer to a boil.

Without mission and persecution, believers rally around programs, gossip, drama, factions, politics, music, children, and whatever else. Believers, like everyone else on the planet, are fallen. If they are not moving in the right direction they disperse and head South.

In the Great Commission, Jesus invites his followers into the plot of history. What he doesn't tell us, what we only find out post-obedience, is that when we embrace the bigger plot, our life suddenly gets plot. That is, we experience a new or heightened sense of drive, drama, purpose, conflict, tension, sorrow, joy, victory, redemption . . . all the ingredients of a great story. I mean, think of the chase scenes, heart-wrenching relationships, harrowing adventures, and dramatic rescues that accompanied the Apostle Paul, all because he's engaged in the mission (the plot).

In lieu of plot, what Christians experience is "drama" in that adolescent-Facebook sense of the word — self-absorbed melodrama. When expansive, forward-moving energy for the plot is suppressed, it comes out sideways in criticalness, discontent, cynicism, boredom, gossip, depression . . . drama. Plot or "drama," one or the other.

**127**

### Attentive to Open Doors and Opportunities

Working in advertising in the 1980s, my agency counted among its clients the US Army. Creative work on the project was contractually kept secret, which was odd because who's going to steal the Army's ad campaign... the Russians? Be that as it may, a 1981 commercial, hugely successful in re-branding the Army's image, featured the tagline, "We do more before 9 a.m. than most people do all day." It's a great line. Almost made you want to get up at 5 a.m. — almost.

The military always has these great slogans that would be perfect for the church: a global force for good (the US Navy), that others may live (Air Force Pararescue), always faithful (the US Marines). I'm not sure what's up with the Finnish Army. According to Wikipedia their slogan is, look good, do good. Got some real dandies in that Finnish Army.

Paul's phrase, making the most of every opportunity, carries a similar ethos, a slogan repeated elsewhere in his letters (Col. 4:5). What is a marine? Always faithful. What is a Christian? Always watchful and attentive for the "opportunity to do good" (Galatians 6:10). This includes the opportunity to encourage, to listen, to serve, to give, to love, to preach, to whatever.

A few weeks ago I talked to my friend Sean on the phone. He sounded exhausted, so I asked him, "What's wrong? You sound awful." Apparently Sean and a couple of friends had gone out to minister to the homeless and one opportunity led to another. Now, here it was three days later and they were living and sleeping on the street with the homeless, still seizing an onslaught of opportunity like Lucille Ball wrapping chocolates on a speeding conveyer belt.

These opportunities to serve and love and pray had existed since the homeless lost their homes, it's just that no one had gone looking for them. I'm a little old to sleep in a cardboard box, so I look for different opportunities than Sean, but he's attentive to God's Spirit in the way I'm trying to be attentive and expectant.

I, as you probably know, work for Cru, and Cru is known for missions and evangelism. It could appear that my promotion of missions and evangelism is due to a Cru-blindness or bias, but I assure you that's not the case. This is simply the physics of the kingdom. Wholeness and spiritual vitality does not come by focusing on fixing ourselves, but in loving and serving others.

Though you may be struggling with purity, do not stop loving and discipling others. Don't put ministry on hold until your life is in order because the quest for wholeness and healing will never be completed. There are two Great Commissions: spreading the gospel to the entire world and spreading the gospel to our entire selves, and both pursuits are optimized in tandem with the other.

### Reflection

Discipleship is basically getting together with someone weekly to grab coffee and check in on what God is teaching and doing in both participants' lives. Are you discipling anyone?

A Bible study a week is good, several are even better. Can you go to or start another?

Have you looked into and prayed about a short-term mission project?

Who is on your top 10 list? By this I mean, who are the ten people you are praying for and looking for opportunity to speak with about Christ?

# NECESSARY PLAN

In his biblical theology that goes by the lengthy title *The Acts of the Risen Lord Jesus, Luke's Account of God's Unfolding Plan*, author Allen Thomson states that "the most prominent term in all of Acts is the greek word dei, which carries the meaning 'it was neccessary.'" Forty times Luke uses the word in Luke-Acts "which is twice as many times as in all 13 of Paul's epistles and significantly more than anywhere else in Scripture."

The point is, or rather Luke's point is, that everything unfolding in the coming of Christ (the spread of the gospel, and the growth of the church) is happening according to a plan. So for example, Luke doesn't just say that the Apostle Paul suffered, but that "he needed" to suffer, and he doesn't just say that Paul went to Rome, but that "it was necessary" for Paul to go to Rome. You get the idea. Because there's a plan, certain things are a necessary part of it.

There is quite a bit of dei, or necessity, in the battle of purity: necessary trials, necessary preparation, necessary community, necessary accountability, necessary growth, et cetera. God has a plan for you and for your life and for your purity and that makes certain things necessary things. What I'm saying is, you need a plan that puts into place those things necessary for your purity. You need to be intentional.

From the articles you've read, the thoughts you've thought, and any affirmations the Lord has given you, what do you need to hold on to? What do you need to put into practice? What do you need to do first or next? What is necessary for you to remember or write down or memorize? In the space below, why don't you try to capture those things?

## JAMES 5:16 GROUPS

**A SEVEN-WEEK COMMUNAL EXPERIMENT —
NOTHING TO HIDE, NOTHING TO LOSE**

Therefore confess your sins to each other and pray for each
other so that you may be healed. The prayer of a righteous
man is powerful and effective.
James 5:16

### An Invitation

If you are already involved in a men's small group, see if the
members would be willing to take a seven-week detour to cover
these important topics. If you don't have a small group, pull together a handful of Christian guys and either lead the Bible study
yourself, or ask someone else to lead.

What follows are seven studies that touch on topics related
to — what else — purity. They're good studies, but the group is
more about relationships — sharing, laughing, and learning to be
open, honest, and vulnerable. The goal is to talk out and live out
this struggle within a grace-filled community of faith. It's hard to
say where the seven weeks will lead you, but you'll move forward
and you'll move further than you would have on your own. This
is a chance to live in a greater freedom and I really hope you'll
take it.

You'll find thoughts and answers to the studies in the back of
the book. Blessings be upon you.

On to the studies...

## WEEK 1: FORGIVEN

---

1. Of all of the sins we commit, nothing makes us feel more guilty than sexual sin. Why do you think that is?

No matter how we've sexually transgressed, we must all agree that nothing is worse than what Peter did. He out right denied Jesus, even after being warned. We can only imagine the sin "hangover" Peter felt from that failure. As a result, there is much we can learn about forgiveness from the account of Peter's restoration.

Read all of John 21:15-24:

> When they had finished eating, Jesus said to Simon Peter, "Simon son of John, do you truly love me more than these?" "Yes, Lord," he said, "you know that I love you." Jesus said, "Feed my lambs." Again Jesus said, "Simon son of John, do you truly love me?" He answered, "Yes, Lord, you know that I love you." Jesus said, "Take care of my sheep." The third time he said to him, "Simon son of John, do you love me?" Peter was hurt because Jesus asked him the third time, "Do you love me? He said, "Lord, you know all things; you know that I love you." Jesus said, "Feed my sheep".
> (v. 15-17)

2. The most obvious question is: Why did Jesus ask Peter three times, "Do you love me?" Is this a rebuke, or an opportunity for confession?

3. Why does Jesus ask Peter if he loves him "more than these?"

4. What are the essential components of confessing our sin? If we are forgiven due to Christ's death, why do we need to confess our sins?

5. What role does faith play in feeling forgiven?

6. Rationalizing, vowing to never commit the same sin again, and berating ourselves: all are human attempts to feel forgiven. How?

7. How is each a betrayal of faith?

8. It took great courage for Peter to hear the painful truth from Jesus. It has been said that courage, or the lack of it, is what keeps us from repentance, growing in holiness, and feeling forgiven. Why? Do you agree? What was the most painful truth you've had to hear about yourself?

> "I tell you the truth, when you were younger you dressed yourself and went where you wanted; but when you are old you will stretch out your hands, and someone else will dress you and lead you where you do not want to go." Jesus said this to indicate the kind of death by which Peter would glorify God. Then he said to him, "Follow me".
> (v. 18-19)

9. What and why is Jesus telling him this?

10. In what way do you think this would have been encouraging to Peter?

11. Is there any application of this for us?

12. Peter has an advantage in that he could see Jesus' face, which must have aided in his feeling forgiven. Who incarnates — or is Jesus' face — for you when you don't feel forgiven?

> Peter turned and saw that the disciple whom Jesus loved was following them. (This was the one who had leaned back against Jesus at the supper and had said, "Lord, who is going to betray you?") When Peter saw him, he asked, "Lord, what about him?" Jesus answered, "If I want him to remain alive until I return, what is that to you? You must follow me".
> (v. 20-22)

13. Why is comparison an enemy of forgiveness?

14. Whose spiritual life puts you under the pile?

15. What struggles do you have that others might not have to deal with?

16. What two things can you do, that you are not doing, to aid in receiving God's forgiveness?

## WEEK 2: LUST

Read 2 Samuel 11:1-4.

In the spring, at the time when kings go off to war, David sent
Joab out with the king's men and the whole Israelite army. They
destroyed the Ammonites and besieged Rabbah. But David re-
mained in Jerusalem. One evening David got up from his bed
and walked around on the roof of the palace. From the roof
he saw a woman bathing. The woman was very beautiful, and
David sent someone to find out about her. The man said, "Isn't
this Bathsheba, the daughter of Eliam and the wife of Uriah the
Hittite?" Then David sent messengers to get her. She came to
him, and he slept with her. (She had purified herself from her uncleanness.) Then she went back home.

1. We all have different things that spark our minds to lust. In his
book *Not Even a Hint*, Joshua Harris calls them "lust triggers."
What do you think might have been some of David's lust triggers?

2. Fill in some of your lust triggers:

When I hear the music of...

When I am feeling particularly...

During this time of day...

When I hang out here...

When I find myself...

After I have just...

3. Is there a lust trigger that you tolerate and make little attempt to guard against? In other words, do you have an allowable form of lust? What is it?

4. What have you chosen to believe about yourself, your situation, or God that makes you allow yourself this freedom?

5. What is the difference between a godly desire for sex, and lust?

6. John Piper makes the statement that, "The fires of lust's pleasures must be fought with the fire of God's pleasures." What does he mean by this?

7. What have you done along these lines?

8. Scripture never mentions masturbation. Do you think we elevate it to a greater sin than it may be? What principles are mentioned in Scripture that masturbation would violate?

9. If it were possible to masturbate without lusting, would it still be sin? Why?

Lowell Seashore in his program, *Lust-Free Living* suggests a tapering down approach in order to stop masturbating. Stage one is to disconnect lust from masturbating. You continue masturbating with a strict discipline of guarding your thoughts. In stage two, you look to cut back on the amount of times you masturbate. Stage three is cutting it out altogether. In contrast, others have stressed a cold turkey approach.

10. Discuss from your own experience the merits, and liabilities of both.

11. How do women's lusts differ from men's? Or do you think there's no difference?

12. Dr. Al Mohler once said, "Men are tempted to give themselves to pornography — women are tempted to commit pornography." Discuss what you think he meant by this.

> But among you there must not be even a hint of sexual immorality, or of any kind of impurity, or of greed, because these are improper for God's holy people.
> Ephesians. 5:3

In seeing victory over lust and masturbation, most Christians agree for the need to make a clear commitment to the standard of "not even a hint," because lust always wants more.

13. Do you think such a standard is attainable?

14. What is the most effective thing you have done to guard yourself against lust?

15. What are the potential problems with making a major covenant or commitment to stop sinning in an area?

16. In light of that, what would be a godly commitment?

17. In your own words, write down your own commitment.

# WEEK 3: TEMPTED

1. Read James 1:13-18. James avoids putting the blame for temptation on Satan. Why?

2. To what extent is Satan involved in our temptation?

In Ephesians 6:11 it says, "Put on the full armor of God so that you can take your stand against the devil's schemes." The Greek word for schemes is noemata, from the root word noema, which means "mind or thought." Not coincidentally, it is also the root of our word noose (as in "hanging"). The word illustrates that Satan's schemes are well conceived and that his temptation efforts are usually confined to the most strategic times, and the most strategic methods.

3. When is it most strategic for Satan to get personally involved with our temptation?

4. How do you know when he's involved? Can you think of a recent time when you felt that he was involved?

5. James 1:14 states, "But each one is tempted when, by his own evil desire, he is dragged away and enticed." As it relates to sex and our desires, what is healthy and godly, and what is evil?

6. Certain temptations are anomalies, but others form consistent themes in our lives. What are your constant temptation themes or scenarios? How have you been tempted recently?

7. James points out that while God provides trials to mature our faith, he never seeks to induce sin to destroy our faith. How might it affect your life if you believed God was tempting you?

> No temptation has seized you except what is common to man. And God is faithful; he will not let you be tempted beyond what you can bear. But when you are tempted, he will also provide a way out so that you can stand up under it.
> 1 Corinthians 10:13

8. According to this verse, not only does God not tempt us, but he provides a means of escape to avoid difficult temptation. If he provides a means of escape, does this mean he doesn't think we can endure it? Are certain temptations, if not avoided, beyond our capacity to decline?

9. When, and how, did God recently provide an escape for you?

10. Why is it critical to remember "that no temptation has seized us," except temptations common to other men?

11. In 1:13 and 17, James conveys God's goodness and care for his children, because at the root of temptation can be a distrust of this truth. Read Genesis 3:1-6 and record what truths Adam and Eve were tempted to distrust.

12. In the midst of temptation, list four lies you are prone to believe about God.

13. In explaining the ritual of temptation, James uses the metaphor of giving birth. In this metaphor, what do you think he means by conception?

Notice that sin does not happen until after conception. Temptation, in and of itself, does not constitute sin. We shouldn't feel we have sinned simply because we are tempted.

14. What temptations make you feel guilty, simply for being tempted?

15. James 1:16 says, "Don't be deceived." What have you learned in this study that would keep you from being deceived? What will you do differently as a result?

# WEEK 4: SEX

1. Read I Thessalonians 4:1-12. Where are the two occurrences of the phrase "more and more" found? What does this tell you about Paul's primary purpose in writing these words?

2. Read verses 3-5 and define the following words:

Sanctified

Sexual immorality

Passionate lust

Heathen

3. What are the specific challenges of our culture to remaining pure until marriage? Do you think we have it better, worse, or the same as others? What is the most difficult of all these factors?

4. Honoring God by controlling our bodies is a consistent theme in Paul's letters. Look up the following verses and record what they say on this issue:

Romans 6:19

Romans 12:1

1 Corinthians 6:13-20

Philippians 1:20-24

5. What insights do these passages give you with regard to
1 Thessalonians 4:3-6?

6. How does sexual immorality wrong or steal from another
brother (or sister)?

7. Imagine you were married, and were having a discussion with
your spouse concerning his or her sexual involvement before
marriage. At what level of physical involvement would you begin
to feel that someone had taken, or stolen, something from you?

8. How important do you feel it is to go back and apologize to
people you have sexually wronged?

Long engagements are fairly common in our culture, which bring
their own complexity. One result is that engaged couples can
easily begin to slide into roles, responsibilities, privileges and intimacy that are proper only when that person belongs to you.

9. How have you witnessed this in relationships you have observed or experienced?

10. Read 1 Thessalonians 4:6-8. What further motivations to remain sexually pure do you see here? In verse 8, why do you think Paul adds the parenthetical phrase "who gives you His Spirit?"

11. Why do you think God wants us to remain sexually pure until marriage?

12. In dating relationships, what levels of physical involvement do you think are clearly off limits? What do you think is allowable? What are some of the gray areas?

13. How have you arrived at this standard?

> Greet one another with a holy kiss. All the churches of Christ send greetings.
> Romans 16:16

> All the brothers here send you greetings. Greet one another with a holy kiss.
> 1 Corinthians. 16:20

14. Some have suggested using the principle of the "Holy Kiss" — showing physical affection with a commitment to not cause sexual arousal. It moves away from a standard of "What can I get away with?" or "How can I avoid all contact?" and says rather, "How can I physically express affection without sexually arousing either myself or partner?" How do you feel about this as a guideline?

# WEEK 5: GROWN

In this study we'll examine how God makes us holy, and shed light on the question: What's God's part in the process, and what's ours?

1. What is the theological word for the process by which we are made holy?


2. The biggest reason we don't see holiness in our lives is that:
- ☐ We don't make right choices
- ☐ We don't have enough faith
- ☐ We don't pray enough
- ☐ We aren't obedient

3. In the spiritual growth process, what would you say is our responsibility? What is God's?


4. Christians can overemphasize either our role or God's. How have you seen this?


A spiritually healthy perspective is one that sees a balance and a partnership as expressed in Philippians 2:12-13:

> Therefore, my dear friends, as you have always obeyed — not only in my presence, but now much more in my absence — continue to work out your salvation with fear and trembling, for it is God who works in you to will and to act according to his good purpose.

5. How have you experienced God's working in you to will and to act according to His purposes?


6. Are there things you can do to increase the Holy Spirit's influence in your life? If so, what?


7. Find a verse that talks about things that hinder the influence or power of the Holy Spirit.


8. What else, besides sin, can hinder our sensitivity to God's Spirit?


9. Philippians 2:12-13 says, "to work out" our salvation. Why isn't this contrary to our salvation being by God's grace alone?


10. We work out (take what God is doing on the inside and put it on the outside) our salvation by habitually making choices, which, over time, change our character. How would you define what a person's character is?


11. In what area of your life have you begun making a new series of choices? What new habits have been created?

12. The question is often asked why God doesn't immediately make us holy. How would you answer that question?


13. In the Scriptures, clearing our lives of sin is similar to the process the Israelites went through in clearing the Promised Land. Read the following passages and write down what insight they give to the last question:

Exodus 23:27, 29


Deuteronomy 6:10-12


Deuteronomy 8:17


14. If you could see anything change in your life immediately, what would it be? Why do you think you have not seen victory yet?


Another reason for the great struggle for holiness is that God wants to teach us how to spiritually fight in partnership with him: "These are the nations the LORD left to test all those Israelites who had not experienced any of the wars in Canaan (he did this only to teach warfare to the descendants of the Israelites who had not had previous battle experience)" (Judges 3:1-2).

15. In your struggle for sexual purity, what are some of the lessons you've learned about fighting this spiritual war?

16. If there is one component more important than others, it is found in Romans 6:12. Look at the verse, and then answer why it is so crucial.


17. Give a passage that affirms the hope that one day the sanctification process will be complete.

# WEEK 6: HELP

The focus of the study is biblical community and accountability. Before we look at community, let's look at its opposite: isolation. Read Mark 5:2-13:

> When Jesus got out of the boat, a man with an evil spirit came from the tombs to meet him. This man lived in the tombs, and no one could bind him any more, not even with a chain. For he had often been chained hand and foot, but he tore the chains apart and broke the irons on his feet. No one was strong enough to subdue him. Night and day among the tombs and in the hills he would cry out and cut himself with stones. When he saw Jesus from a distance, he ran and fell on his knees in front of him. He shouted at the top of his voice,

> "What do you want with me, Jesus, Son of the Most High God? Swear to God that you won't torture me!" For Jesus had said to him, "Come out of this man, you evil spirit!" Then Jesus asked him, "What is your name?"

> "My name is Legion," he replied, "for we are many." And he begged Jesus again and again not to send them out of the area.

> A large herd of pigs was feeding on the nearby hillside. The demons begged Jesus, "Send us among the pigs; allow us to go into them." He gave them permission, and the evil spirits came out and went into the pigs. The herd, about two thousand in number, rushed down the steep bank into the lake and were drowned.

1. Do you think isolation led to this man's state? Or, was his state caused by isolation?

2. How does isolation give Satan a foothold in our lives?

3. What causes people to isolate themselves? What causes you to isolate yourself from others?

4. Isolated and attacked, the man's mind became obsessed with death (living in tombs), self-destruction (cutting himself), and with the profane and perverse (not wearing clothes). How are your mind and thinking impaired by isolation?

5. Having spent too much time alone, what is the most bizarre thing you've begun to ponder?

6. In your experience, do media outlets (movies, music, computers, etc) relieve isolation or increase it?

7. The opposite of isolation is accountability and community. On a scale from 1 to 10, how would you rate your experience of community? Of isolation?

8. How would you define Christian community?

9. The reason we need community is that we all need to be known. Speaking of which, share one thing with the group that

you have never told anyone else about yourself.

In the area of sexual immorality, one of the great benefits of community is found in this verse:

> Therefore, confess your sins to each other and pray for each other so that you may be healed.
> James 5:16

10. How does confessing our sins to others lead to healing?

11. What is different about this passage from 1 John 1:9?

The 12-step Alcoholics Anonymous program was founded on Christian principles. Most people who make it through the program cite Step 5 as the most critical step. It states: "Admitted to God, to ourselves and to another human being the exact nature of our wrongs."

12. Step 5 is essentially James 5:16. With whom can you, or do you, share the exact nature of your wrongs?

13. The term used for Christian friendships that help one another in the area of sexual purity is "accountability." What does accountability mean?

14. What sorts of things might you do to hold one another accountable?


15. It has been said that a true accountability partner models both "grace and truth." What do you think this means? Who models this for you?


16. Do you tend to be more grace- or more truth-oriented?


In Hebrews 10:24 it says, "And let us consider how we may spur one another on toward love and good deeds."

17. Who could you spur on? List three things you could do that would spur a friend on to love and good deeds?

# WEEK 7: TRUTH

The power of lust is a lie. Yet, with Christ in our hearts, we cannot endure the pain of outright rebellion. So, to do the unthinkable, we conceal ideas under layers of lies, smuggling in lust dressed in rationales, justifications and outright lies.

1. Write out five justifications for giving in momentarily to sex or pornography.

**1.**

**2.**

**3.**

**4.**

**5.**

2. When the word "truth" is used in the Bible it can have different shades of meaning. What does truth mean in each of these passages:

> Then you will know the truth, and the truth will set you free.
> John 8:32

> An instructor of the foolish, a teacher of infants, because you have in the law the embodiment of knowledge and truth.
> Romans 2:20

> Love does not delight in evil but rejoices with the truth.
> 1 Corinthians 13:6

> Instead, speaking the truth in love, we will in all things grow up into him who is the Head, that is, Christ.
> Ephesians 4:15

Surely you heard of him and were taught in him in accordance with the truth that is in Jesus.
Ephesians 4:21

3. As a lifestyle, where are you most prone to exaggerate or stretch the truth? With whom? Why?

4. In John 8:32 it says, "Then you will know the truth, and the truth will set you free." Can you think of a time when speaking or telling the truth brought with it a sense of freedom?

5. Why does truth make us feel free?

"But what about you?" he asked. "Who do you say I am?" Peter answered, "You are the Christ." Jesus warned them not to tell anyone about him. He then began to teach them that the Son of Man must suffer many things and be rejected by the elders, chief priests and teachers of the law, and that he must be killed and after three days rise again. He spoke plainly about this, and Peter took him aside and began to rebuke him. But when Jesus turned and looked at his disciples, he rebuked Peter. "Get behind me, Satan!"
Mark 8:29-33

6. What is it about Peter's words that would be a temptation to Jesus?

7. Notice Jesus does not respond with Scripture, but how does he use truth as a weapon?

8. Think of two ways you could use the power of total truth and honesty to help you fight against lust and pornography.

**1.**
**2.**

9. Vulnerability is one form of truth. Write down a precise summary of the truth of your sexual temptation, history, struggle, failure and success.

Now you have a choice whether you want to read this to the group right now or not, but it should not be a choice of whether or not you keep this to yourself. Disclosing the truth will set you free.

### The Truth of Scripture

10. What is different about the truth of Scripture from the general truthfulness we have been talking about?

In Joshua Harris' book, *Not Even a Hint* he says, "Part of sin is dissatisfaction with God. Lust's power comes from the promise it gives that something besides God can make us happy. What this means is the only way to overcome the power of lust in our lives is by finding better promises."

11. Can you think of better promises found in Scripture?

12. What passages have you memorized related to your battle against lust? How has it helped and what passage has been most helpful? How do you memorize them?

> Consequently, faith comes from hearing the message, and the message is heard through the word of Christ.
> Romans 10:17

13. Scripture is not clear on this point, but some have suggested that during temptation it is more powerful to say aloud the Scripture than simply think it. This is hard to deny or confirm. What do you think?

> Flee from sexual immorality. All other sins a man commits are outside his body, but he who sins sexually sins against his own body. Do you not know that your body is a temple of the Holy Spirit, who is in you, whom you have received from God? You are not your own; you were bought at a price. Therefore honor God with your body.
> 1 Corinthians 6:18-20

14. Scripture is not magic. Speaking it out loud doesn't make lust go away. What does determine, or enhance, the efficacy of Scripture?

15. What is one thing you will do this week to utilize truth in your fight against lust?

## 28 DAYS LATER

**A One Month Devotional on Purity and Sex, Grace and Truth**

Your devotional time is about knowing and growing in the Lord, which can be the problem with topical devotionals: they can focus the heart and mind on ideas, issues, and ourselves, rather than the Lord. I say this because this is a topical devotional and I don't want the subject of purity to eclipse your relationship with Christ. The point of this devotional section is to pull out biblical concepts discussed in the articles and give you time to process them with the Lord. If you do that then I think it will be fruitful, allowing God to personalize the content and you to integrate it.

> My son, pay attention to my wisdom, listen well to my words of insight,
> That you may maintain discretion and your lips may preserve knowledge.
> For the lips of an adulteress drip honey, and her speech is smoother than oil;
> But in the end she is bitter as gall, sharp as a double-edged sword.
> Her feet go down to death; her steps lead straight to the grave.
> She gives no thought to the way of life; her paths are crooked, but she knows it not.
> Now then, my sons, listen to me; do not turn aside from what I say.
> Keep to a path far from her, do not go near the door of her house.
> Proverbs 5:1-8

### DAY 1

> I made a covenant with my eyes not to look lustfully at a girl.
> Job 31:1

Have you ever tried to this? Make a covenant in your heart not to lust? "Difficult" would be an understatement. What makes it doubly difficult is "the power of the law." That power is often activated whenever we vow to NOT, NOT do something. Trying to "not lust" can make us think about lust *even* more. But with the Spirit of the New Covenant inside us, the dynamic of spiritual growth is more relational (you talking to God about things) and directed more toward the positive: "how we can better love and care for women" vs. "How we can stop lusting after women."

Our thought life is crucial, and the best way to keep our thoughts in line is to keep them in prayer. So when the beauty of someone strikes you, talk to the Lord about it. Ask God to help you to honestly pray for them. Ask God to help you not to worship their beauty. Focus your heart and attention toward the woman, or women, who seem left out, and don't receive much male attention. Make their day. When the apostle Paul says to "set your minds on the things above" I think this is the sort of thing he is talking about. Covenant to love better.

## DAY 2

> As Jesus went on from there, two blind men followed him,
> calling out, "Have mercy on us, Son of David!" When he had
> gone indoors, the blind men came to him, and he asked
> them, "Do you believe that I am able to do this?" "Yes, Lord,"
> they replied. Then he touched their eyes and said,
> "According to your faith will it be done to you."
> Matthew 9:27-29

You're a hopeless case when it comes to lust, or at least that's what you've come to believe, and — no offense — for good reason. Your efforts to quit lusting, or masturbating, or whatever, haven't seen stellar results, so the thought of a lust-free life seems beyond reasonable expectation.

But speaking of "beyond all reasonable expectation," consider this blind man. Having never seen your entire life, could you imagine believing that Jesus could, in an instant, make you see? Why stop there? Why not ask Jesus to fly? It's no less impossible.

Jesus recognizes the great faith exerted by the man, and because of it, grants his request. What made the blind man's faith so great was that his request was beyond all reasonable expectation.

Because Jesus has much to teach us through our struggle with lust, he favors time and process in our healing. But in and through the duration, we need to cling to faith, believing that God can and will lead us to victory. What is tested and taxed most in the journey toward purity is not discipline, but faith — continuing to trust God beyond all reasonable expectation. In your relational and sexual struggles, how and where does God want you to exert faith?

"Dear Diary, today I touched myself..."

Rule number two about keeping a devotional journal is, don't let anyone read it. Rule number one is, you need to get a devotional journal. Just pick up any spiral bound thing, and no, don't use your phone/watch/computer/robot to journal; wrap your hand around a pen. Listen to these words:

> When I kept silent, my bones wasted away through my groaning all day long. For day and night your hand was heavy upon me; my strength was sapped as in the heat of summer. Then I acknowledged my sin to you and did not cover up my iniquity. I said, "I will confess my transgressions to the LORD" — and you forgave the guilt of my sin.
> Psalm 32:3-5

If you think about it, the Psalms are really David's journal, put to music. But don't put yours to music because no one wants to hear a song entitled, "Today, I touched myself." A journal helps you to process your thoughts and emotions with God. As you see in Psalm 32, it can also help in experiencing God's grace. Chronicling achieves the effect of focus: keeping attention on areas that need attention, prayer, processing, and grace. Areas like purity.

## DAY 4

Wisdom will save you from the ways of wicked men, from men whose words are perverse, It will save you also from the adulteress, from the wayward wife with her seductive words, who has left the partner of her youth and ignored the covenant she made before God. For her house leads down to death and her paths to the spirits of the dead. None who go to her return or attain the paths of life.
Proverbs 2:12-14, 19

The book of Proverbs is a collection of wise sayings and general truisms collected or composed by King David's son, Solomon. Proverbs are a template for wise living; a generic template not burdened by anomalies or exceptions, but the general rule. Such is the genre of wisdom literature, which often contrasts wisdom with its opposite, folly or foolishness.

As you know by experience, and as Proverbs points out in considerable detail, sex and lust have a breathtaking capacity to make us act like fools. So, supplementing whatever else you're reading in your devotional times, try to spend time each day in Proverbs as you journey toward purity. More than anything, it will stir a passion for wisdom and loathing for folly. And lust is folly. Start today in Proverbs 1, and write down your thoughts in your new journal.

Now that you have purified yourselves by obeying the truth
so that you have sincere love for your brothers, love one
another deeply, from the heart.
1 Peter 1:22

One of the ugly side effects of pornography is it leads to the sexualizing, and dehumanizing, of women. It's a terrible lens through
which to view our sisters in Christ. When our mind views women
as a sexual apparatus, we do not see them as they truly are, as
God made them. We do not see in them the image of God but
an image of our own making to serve and worship us — an idol.
Talk about this with God. Tell him about specific women you've
failed to love and ask him to help you see them as he sees them,
to care for them as he cares for them. Take time to memorize this
verse in 1 Peter: *Now that you have purified yourselves by obeying
the truth so that you have sincere love for your brothers, love one
another deeply, from the heart.*

## DAY 6

Therefore, confess your sins to each other and pray for each other so that you may be healed. The prayer of a righteous man is powerful and effective.

James 5:16

In 1 John 1:9 it says that if we confess our sins, He will cleanse us from all unrighteousness. So, we've got that working for us, which is nice. But this passage in James speaks of healing and not cleansing, getting well, not feeling better. In other words, the residual effect of confessing to God is cleansing from sin; the residual effect of confessing to others is getting better.

In this book, and this study, we've focused a lot on ourselves — unavoidably so. But in love we need to think of those around us: brothers in Christ who may be burdened with guilt and shame from sexual sin, living in isolation and defeat.

Who could you reach out to this week? Grab coffee with them, and, if appropriate, share some of your struggles in the area of purity. Not for your benefit, but theirs. You want to share with the hope that your vulnerability will be reciprocated — that, in turn, your friend would open up and find great freedom in doing so. As it says in Galatians 6:2, "Carry each other's burdens, and in this way you will fulfill the law of Christ." Pray about whose burden you might help carry.

> Therefore put on the full armor of God, so that when the day
> of evil comes, you may be able to stand your ground, and
> after you have done everything, to stand. Stand firm then,
> with the belt of truth buckled around your waist,
> with the breastplate of righteousness in place, and with
> your feet fitted with the readiness that comes from the
> gospel of peace.
> Ephesians 6:13-15

In focusing on lust-free living, our spiritual life can start to re-semble therapy: Scripture becoming inkblots into which we only see our personal struggles. What you notice in the above passage is an important part of the armor of God is a willingness to be a witness.

Evangelism is outward focused — other focused — and avails us to the power of God's Spirit. That empowerment backwashes into every area of our spiritual life. Being a witness to the resurrected Christ catalyzes the entire Christian life. Remember that. When you least feel like reaching out, or least qualified, it's often a very good time to minister to others. There are other battles besides your own and an important one is happening right now in the lives of your unbelieving friends.

Today, focus your prayer on friends or family that don't know Jesus. Write down the names of five of them below, and for each, ask the Lord, not only for their salvation, but how he might use you in the process.

## DAY 8

> But among you there must not be even a hint of sexual immorality, or of any kind of impurity, or of greed, because these are improper for God's holy people.
> Ephesians 5:3

The flesh is always looking for a foothold, and if it can't, get that it will settle for a toe-hold. In the journey toward purity, one of the detours is allowing allowable lust. By allowable lust, I mean something not gross or overt, something "relatively harmless" that is lust nonetheless.

In a conversation I had with a Christian brother, he shared with me that he had stopped going to hardcore websites and that the worst thing he watched was infomercials for some Girls-Gone-Wild kind of thing. He's seeing progress, which is great. But, do you see how easy it is to have allowable lust — a few photos in the scrapbook from another life?

Like poker, lust can just sort of hang around — not a threat but still in the game — until things turn around suddenly, and lust starts winning the game. That's why Paul encourages the Ephesians to avoid even a hint of sexual immorality. A hint becomes a rumor, becomes a full-fledged lie. Pray and ask God to reveal any areas where you're allowing allowable lust, and don't allow it.

> For this very reason, make every effort to add to your faith goodness; and to goodness, knowledge; and to knowledge, self-control; and to self-control, perseverance; and to perseverance, godliness; and to godliness, brotherly kindness; and to brotherly kindness, love. For if you possess these qualities in increasing measure, they will keep you from being ineffective and unproductive in your knowledge of our Lord Jesus Christ.
> 2 Peter 1:5-8

Scripture captures here the importance of movement and power of momentum. Momentum is a thing. Success is marked by forward movement, no matter how far back your starting point or whether your progress is measured in inches instead of feet. In an area like masturbation, progress can be seen in the infrequency you give in, or in stopping yourself in the midst of the act.

Growth is growth. Progress is progress. Look for progress and avoid stark categories like "success" and "failure." Don't be discouraged by partial failure because it's also a partial victory, just as long as you're moving forward. Take time to reflect on what progress you've seen and where God has brought you so far in the journey. Thank him for the progress and the partial victories. God is not frustrated by the speed and process of change; he invented time.

Writer and pastor John Piper once said that, "the fires of lust's pleasures must be fought with the fire of God's pleasures." I like that and not because it rhymes but rather in spite of it. Worship, focusing our hearts and minds on the greatness of God, is far and away the greatest medicine for the heart, the greatest antidote for lust. When we are truly worshipping, our hearts see the beauty of God and the ugliness of our idols. Only worship can bring such a change of perspective and affection. Yet getting our hearts to a state of worship is a challenge. If only we could turn on a switch, like a light, but unfortunately worship is a fire that has to be kindled.

There are different points of entrance to a state of worship. Thanksgiving is the most accessible for me, so lets do that. As you begin to give thanks and then keep giving thanks, at some point it starts gushing out on its own, like priming a pump. So start by listing 20 things you are truly thankful for, and, having cultivated thankfulness in your heart, you just keep on going, giving thanks for everything the Spirit brings to mind.

> In the spring, at the time when kings go off to war, David
> sent Joab out with the king's men and the whole Israelite
> army. They destroyed the Ammonites and besieged Rabbah.
> But David remained in Jerusalem. One evening David got up
> from his bed and walked around on the roof of the palace.
> From the roof he saw a woman bathing. The woman was very
> beautiful, and David sent someone to find out about her. The
> man said, "Isn't this Bathsheba, the daughter of Eliam and
> the wife of Uriah the Hittite?" Then David sent messengers to
> get her. She came to him, and he slept with her.
> 2 Samuel 11:1-4

Bored, hanging around rather than going to war, up late at night, walking on the rooftop, spying, staring lustfully: those are some volatile ingredients to mix together. The result of sexual sin was hardly a surprise, more of an expectation. We can find ourselves in the very same mental state (or trance), staring at a glowing screen on our phone or computer.

Once the gears of lust start grinding, it's near impossible to shut down the machine. In the description of 2 Samuel, Scripture clearly wants us to see that David put himself in that vulnerable situation, assuming he'd be fine or hoping that he wouldn't.

Comb through your life in prayer right now and ask God to reveal where you are leaving yourself vulnerable to temptation. Ask him what steps you should be taking to protect yourself, and for the conviction to do so.

## DAY 12

One day as [Jesus] was teaching, Pharisees and teachers of
the law, who had come from every village of Galilee and from
Judea and Jerusalem, were sitting there. And the power of
the Lord was present for him to heal the sick.
Luke 5:17

In the story of Jesus healing the paralytic, you could easily
miss this phrase: "And the power of the Lord was present for
him to heal the sick." Luke show us that Jesus — though being
God — relied continually on the Holy Spirit to perform mighty
works and accomplish the Father's will. Jesus modeled for us an
*abiding* life.

We do not simply go out and do things for God, but as we abide
in His Spirit, He leads us in His will and empowers us to carry it
out. Abiding is connectedness: constantly drawing upon God's
strength and wisdom throughout the day: *Lord, give me strength;
Lord, show me what I should say; show me what to do.* Constant
abiding and dependence is how we access God's power to live a
life pleasing to Him. Be conscious of abiding today — conscious-
ly abide.

> Stand firm then, with the belt of truth buckled around your
> waist, with the breastplate of righteousness in place...
> Ephesians 6:14

In this passage, the apostle Paul tells us that a life of truth and
godliness leaves little foothold for temptation. Because the power
of lust is a lie, being and staying in the truth is a powerful defense
against it. Honesty moves in three directions: being honest with
God, with yourself, and with others.

Pray and ask God to reveal any areas of your life where you are
less than truthful or lacking genuine integrity. Ask God to reveal
lies you are believing in the realm of sex and lust, and commit to
God your desire to stay within the light of complete truthfulness
and self disclosure. Truth is a protective firewall around your
heart and mind, so for no reason compromise or damage it. If you
do, fix it. Go back and tell the complete truth.

## DAY 14

> For this reason a man will leave his father and mother and be
> united to his wife, and they will become one flesh.
> Genesis 2:24

To this day I feel guilty when I say the word "butt." Like most adolescents butt constituted a significant part of my vocabulary. There was something rebellious and scandalous and enticing about this hidden part of the anatomy. Of course, given the right context, there's nothing morally wrong with the part of the human body known as the "butt."

Something similar happens with sex, as we become more conscious of sexual sin and immorality. Sex takes on the property of "being dirty." But of course there's nothing dirty about sex in the right context. Our sin and perversion is dirty, God's creation of sex is brilliant and beautiful.

Take time to reflect on the beauty and genius of sex and marriage and gender. Praise God for his unimaginable creativity. Ask him to restore in you an untainted vision of physical intimacy. Dialogue with him about the specific ways and peculiar fetishes your heart and mind have conceived. Ask him for insight into these twists and turns. Thank him for your healthy attraction and desire for intimacy.

## DAY 15

Do you not know that your body is a temple of the Holy
Spirit, who is in you, whom you have received from God? You
are not your own...
1 Corinthians 6:19

It is due to Jesus' immeasurable sacrifice that our sins have been
forgiven, but that's not the point of this verse. The point is to
make us aware that another member of the Trinity also suffers
when we sin, particularly in the sexual area. Because the Holy
Spirit is in us, when we bring lust into our hearts and minds, we
are also bringing it into the very Temple of God. It's like showing
pornography on the walls of a church.

Take time to tell the Holy Spirit how sorry you are for all the
times and ways you've treated his sanctuary dishonorably.
Scripture tells us not to "grieve God's Spirit" and if God's Spirit can
be grieved, there's no question we've done it. Apologize for the
grief you've caused him, and thank him for his patient endurance
of your sin. Ask him to help you keep his dwelling place holy.

Do not judge, and you will not be judged. Do not condemn, and you will not be condemned. Forgive, and you will be forgiven. Give, and it will be given to you. A good measure, pressed down, shaken together and running over, will be poured into your lap. For with the measure you use, it will be measured to you.
Luke 6:37-38

Feeling forgiven and experiencing God's grace are inextricably tied to the forgiveness and grace we show others. If we are not forgiving others, we will have a hard time experiencing God's forgiveness, for we reflexively attribute to God and his judgments the standards we impose on others. If we force others to experience the consequence of their sin, we should not expect a get out of jail free card when our sin brings painful consequences. In dating, in sex, and in relationships in general, there is ample opportunity to exercise forgiveness.

Going back through relationships you've had and have, who do you need to forgive? Who has hurt you or wronged you or embarrassed you or abused you? Who do you need to forgive with the forgiveness you yourself have received? You may want to write down some names or things below.

> For it is shameful even to mention what the disobedient do in secret. But everything exposed by the light becomes visible...
> Ephesians 5:12-13

Like a tire to potholes and my iPhone to pavement, I feel an inextricable attraction to the lives of "the disobedient." In contrast to this verse, my flesh is terribly curious about what the disobedient have been up to and with whom, and media makes its money by finding out and reporting it to me. My eyes and ears cling to lustful fragments of conversations and news stories, and shards of images and innuendo get lodged in my mind. Much is not in our power to avoid, because filth is everywhere. But some is, and we need to be vigilant to guard our heart and mind from what the disobedient are doing. What are some actions you could or should take to protect yourself from lustful pollution?

One day he went into the house to attend to his duties, and none of the household servants was inside. She caught him by his cloak and said, "Come to bed with me!" But he left his cloak in her hand and ran out of the house.
Genesis 39:11-12

To me, what's most memorable about the story of Joseph is not that he resisted temptation, admirable as that is, but according to the Genesis narrative, he ended up going to prison for it.

After making good choices about lust and relationships, we have an expectation of reward in an obvious, immediate, and tangible way. When trouble follows trials, it can provide our flesh justification for returning to sin.

Because of this dynamic and the nature of spiritual battle, you'll do well to expect that obedience will often be met with opposition, not affirmation. Remember that trials are an indicator, not that we are doing something wrong, but that we are doing something right. The trial itself is affirmation.

> This, then, is how you should pray: "Our Father in heaven,
> hallowed be your name ... and lead us not into temptation,
> but deliver us from the evil one."
> Matthew 6:9,13

While everyone knows this model prayer Jesus taught his disciples, I wonder if something gets lost in the familiarity. I always pray for forgiveness and God's will, but I almost never pray to be spared temptation.

Maybe it's because, when I do pray, I never see what I'm spared from. Maybe it's because I wrongly assume that I don't have any say in the matter. Whatever the reason, it's clear from Jesus' words that not only do I have a vote, but I'm supposed to vote. If Jesus told us to pray daily and pray for protection from temptation, then we should probably do it. It must make a difference.

This is an important principle that I continually forget and Scripture continually reminds me: never *presume* God's active involvement; *pray* for it.

**DAY 20**

"So I say to you: Ask and it will be given to you; seek and you will find; knock and the door will be opened to you."
Luke 11:9

What's the difference between hitting a door and knocking on it? Repetition. In this section of Luke, Jesus is teaching some important lessons on prayer, one of which is perseverance.

Faith is not simply measured by its intensity (zeal), but by its duration. Suppose I leave, promising I'll return soon. And imagine after only a day, you stop looking out the window. You'd have to question whether you really believed what I told you.

Our continuing to come to God in prayer, seeking what we desire, not only expresses faith, it actually grows our faith. Over time, faith kneads out into something larger than the original lump. There are many reasons God values perseverance in our prayers, but the important thing is that he does. No matter how many times you've prayed in the past about lust, relationships, a wife, pornography, etc: keep pounding at the door. In God's timing, it will be opened to you.

Therefore, as God's chosen people, holy and dearly loved, clothe yourselves with compassion, kindness, humility, gentleness and patience. Bear with each other and forgive whatever grievances you may have against one another. Forgive as the Lord forgave you.
Colossians 3:12-13

Here is a correlation to watch for: As self-discipline grows, our grace to others can diminish. We find ourselves thinking: "I got my life together, why can't he?" You might not say it, or even fully form the thought, but it's there.

As you grow in purity and as God brings victory, always come back in your heart and thoughts to who you'd be without Christ, what you've been forgiven for, and what he's delivered you out of. One of the fruits of humbling ourselves is the continued ability to forgive and extend grace to others. If there is one encouragement and blessing that comes from sexual failure — and there may be only *one* — it's humility as well as freedom from pretense, judging, and pride.

## DAY 22

> Here a great number of disabled people used to lie — the blind, the lame, the paralyzed. One who was there had been an invalid for thirty-eight years. When Jesus saw him lying there and learned that he had been in this condition for a long time, he asked him, "Do you want to get well?"
> John 5:3-6

Do you want to get well? Somehow I can't picture anyone responding, "Hmm, let me think about that and get back to you." It seems like a dumb question. It's not.

After years of living with any deficiency, it tends to define your life and your identity. Imagine if you were this blind man. What would happen when you received your sight? You'd have to work. Get a career. Find a skill. Pull your weight in the community. Do things yourself and no longer have any excuses. You would have to assume a whole new identity.

So Jesus doesn't ask, "Do you want to feel well?" He asks, "Do you want to get well?" All that to say, our heart has reasons for remaining in sin and Jesus' question surfaces that issue. Some of our long-suffering with lust is God's plan for deeply changing our hearts, helping us *desire* to "get well." Thank God for his unseen and under-appreciated work in changing your heart. Pray that God would strengthen your resolve to actually be well (holy and pure).

The teachers of the law and the Pharisees brought in a woman caught in adultery. They made her stand before the group and said to Jesus, "Teacher, this woman was caught in the act of adultery. In the Law Moses commanded us to stone such women. Now what do you say?" They were using this question as a trap, in order to have a basis for accusing him. But Jesus bent down and started to write on the ground with his finger. When they kept on questioning him, he straightened up and said to them, "If any one of you is without sin, let him be the first to throw a stone at her." Again he stooped down and wrote on the ground. At this, those who heard began to go away one at a time, the older ones first, until only Jesus was left, with the woman still standing there. Jesus straightened up and asked her, "Woman, where are they? Has no one condemned you?" "No one, sir," she said. "Then neither do I condemn you," Jesus declared. "Go now and leave your life of sin."
John 8:3-11

One could easily get swept up in speculation as to what Jesus was writing on the ground. John tells us not once, but twice, that he was writing 'on the ground with his finger.' But in pondering what he wrote, one we could miss the point entirely.

The Old Testament describes, with the same peculiar detail, that God gave the Law to Moses by inscribing on a stone... "with his finger." The imagery John is describing and Jesus is enacting, is that he is the ultimate Giver of the Law. Absurdly, the Jewish experts in the Law were confronting the very author of the Law, on some issue of the Law.

So, the author of the moral law of the universe is brought a woman guilty of sexual immorality, and what does he do? He forgives her. He releases her from the Law's guilt, condemnation, and judgment. Who were they to condemn the woman, when he had pardoned her? And for that matter, who are we to condemn ourselves when God has pardoned us? If you've sinned and confessed your sin to the Lord, you are free to go. Take some time to confess any sins the Lord brings to mind, and then thank him that you are free to go.

## DAY 24

What shall we say, then? Shall we go on sinning so that grace may increase? By no means! We died to sin; how can we live in it any longer? Or don't you know that all of us who were baptized into Christ Jesus were baptized into his death? We were therefore buried with him through baptism into death in order that, just as Christ was raised from the dead through the glory of the Father, we too may live a new life.
Romans 6:1-4

There's a lot of theology in this passage — so much so that it's easy to miss the big picture. Here's what that picture is: Christ's death was your death as he took your place, dying for your sins. But the reverse is also true: now your life is his life. The resurrected Jesus desires to live his life in and through you. Like a shot of espresso, let this thought reorient you each morning as you wake. The resurrected Christ desires to live his life in and through you today.

With eyes of faith, go through your day looking and seeking God's guidance. Trust that he will lead you. Trust that he has an agenda for your day. This is critical to the "Spirit-filled" life, which is critical to a life of purity.

When all the people were being baptized, Jesus was baptized too. And as he was praying, heaven was opened and the Holy Spirit descended on him in bodily form like a dove. And a voice came from heaven: "You are my Son, whom I love; with you I am well pleased."
Luke 3:21-22

The Gospels bring out many aspects of the relationship between Jesus and His Father. This one is either taken for granted or overlooked. The Father is well pleased by the Son, and the Son lives to please His Father — not simply to obey, but to please. Obeying and pleasing are different, and the nuance leads us to reflect: Am I pleasing God? Is He happy with me, does He like me? Obedience and love are words with different feels to them. We know God loves us — He kind of has to — but does He like us? The feeling of being pleasing, not simply loved or obedient, comes through intimacy. Only in day-to-day closeness does our nagging sense that God is not "for us" disappear. No amount of obedience apart from that intimacy can produce the same sense. Holiness, purity, ministry: the Christian life is filled with many important activities and goals but the one that matters most is pursuing intimacy with the Lord. If you never lusted again and yet were distant from the Lord, it would mean little. Keep intimacy with Christ the main thing. Always.

## DAY 26

> Therefore, prepare your minds for action; be self-controlled;
> set your hope fully on the grace to be given you when Jesus
> Christ is revealed. As obedient children, do not conform to
> the evil desires you had when you lived in ignorance. But just
> as he who called you is holy, so be holy in all you do; for it is
> written: "Be holy, because I am holy."
> 1 Peter 1:13-16

Peter, concerned for his flock, wants to take their minds off their
present struggle and put it on the future, creating hope. There are
many things about the future that provide powerful encouragement for obedience and purity today, but here are the top three:
don't you want your marriage and family to be the very best;
don't you want to have the most intimate walk with Christ possible; and, don't you want to be fully rewarded by the Lord (whatever that may look like)?

These are the potential realities that your obedience today can
bring about. The power of hope is that it keeps us persevering
when there's no comfort or relief presently available. Write down
some other realities and rewards that you'd like to stick on your
mind's refrigerator door, to keep handy when your endurance is
wearing thin.

> But because of his great love for us, God, who is rich in mercy...
> Ephesians 2:4

Rationalizing, justifying and condemning ourselves for sexual sin would make enormous sense if the Bible was littered with phrases like: "All praise to our semi-merciful God. God, ever-present, but emotionally detached," or, "God the quasi-merciful one." Rather, Scripture is filled with phrases like this one, that not only state that God is merciful, but that he is wealthy beyond measure with the commodity — the stuff is just falling out of his pockets! Experiencing and enjoying forgiveness is an issue of faith. You simply must believe Scripture when it says that your sins are forgiven and God's "mercies are new every morning." Though today you may have completely taken his mercy to the bank, there is a fresh supply tomorrow, a bottomless piggy bank. To bolster your faith, do a word search in your Bible concordance on God's mercy and loving-kindness.

> Therefore do not let sin reign in your mortal body so that you
> obey its evil desires.
> Romans 6:12

As Christians, we are quick to make vows, and part of the reason is that it relieves our conscience.

The remorse of failure is assuaged by the belief that the future will hold a better performance.

Unfortunately, the ability to make good on such vows falls outside of our capacity to ensure, and failure only heightens our guilt. In light of this, it's best to stay clear of such vows. But, the Bible does call us to make commitments, not to win (which we cannot promise) but to fight (which is within our power). We are to say, "I will never give in to this sin and I will fight for its removal with all of my and God's resources." It is critical that on this point we vow that we will not let the sin of lust set up its kingdom in our lives, or accept it as "the way things are." In this sense it is not so much a vow as a declaration to fight and never give in. Perhaps you'd like to state your own declaration below:

## LEADER'S GUIDES

### Week 1: Forgiven

1. Part of the answer may be cultural: sexual sins bring the most condemnation. It might be physical, something about the raw and fleshly nature of the act. And last, sex involves a very deep part of us. Failure in this area seems to go right to our core.

2. Jesus repeats the question three times because Peter denied him three times. This is an opportunity for confession, to repeat, "I love you" for every time he had denied it. It is important to see that Jesus is helping Peter to feel forgiven and restored, not rubbing salt in a wound.

3. If you look at the account, just prior to his betrayal, Peter claims that even if all the disciples fall away, he would not. Peter was claiming a greater level of commitment. Here, Jesus is reminding him that his true failure was not the denial but the pride that precipitated it.

4. The essential components include: acknowledging that we have sinned, acknowledging that Jesus' death has paid for our sin and that all is forgiven and then turning from a path of sin to God in repentance. While sin does not hinder our relationship with God, just like in a family, it hinders fellowship.

5. We can confess our sin, but if we don't trust in God's Word and his incredible mercy, we will still feel he is angry with us. We must believe that what the Bible says is true.

6. Read the article "The Place of Faith" for a detailed answer. All are human ways to aid us in feeling forgiven: trusting in our ability to obey in the future; minimizing the sin so it will be easier for God to forgive; or berating ourselves to help pay for the sin. These are alternatives to faith, which choose to believe that we are forgiven no matter what we've done because of Christ.

7. See question six.

8. A major reason we do not grow in holiness is because we don't have the courage to hear painful truth about ourselves from God, our conscience or others. When we filter out hurtful truth, we spare ourselves pain. But, that pain is the needed fuel of repentance. Repentance, in turn, leads to growth. True repentance also helps us to feel forgiven. See the article called "Forgiven."

9. Jesus is telling Peter that he will have a second chance to prove his allegiance and love through martyrdom and that the next time he won't fail.

10. It's a lot like a half-time pep talk from a football coach, saying, "There's a whole second half of this game to play. Put the failure behind you and get back on the field, because we're going to win this game."

11. No matter how many times we fail, God gives us a second chance. God doesn't want us sidelined from the Christian life because of a moral failure.

12. Discuss who provides accountability in the sexual area for each member of the group.

13. Comparing ourselves to others becomes the basis for our forgiveness, not God's forgiveness and mercy. This is what fueled the judgmental hearts of the Pharisees.

14. Discuss as a group.

15. The point you want to bring out here is that everyone has a different race to run. No one knows how difficult certain areas might be for others, nor how easy. No one knows the background or emotional make-up of others, all of which factor into our outward spiritual performance.

16. Look for people to make two solid action points.

At the end of your time, you might give an opportunity to anyone struggling to feel forgiven to share his sin and struggle with the group. Then have the group pray for the individual. This might really minister to that person.

## Week 2: Lust

In preparation for the study, read the articles "I'm Bored" and "Plan of Action."

1. Some of David's lust triggers included walking on the roof, spying on women bathers, being alone and being bored.

2. Share some of your own examples to get the group going. Feel free to add more categories.

3. Try to bring out the fact that most people have one or two areas where they let their guard down and allow their minds to fantasize.

4. At the heart of these tiny sins is usually some form of rationalization. We tell ourselves, "It's much better than other things I could be doing. I'm not having sex. God knows I'm a man."

5. Lust literally means "over passion" and refers to thinking through the activity to the point where you feel compelled to act out in some way. A normal desire is to want to have sex. Lust is actually fantasizing about it.

6. We will never see success against lust if our battle plan is simply to stop. Our desires need godly alternatives. We must fan to flame our passion toward God. We replace lust with greater worship and experience of God.

7. Share some ways you have experienced intimacy with God. Read the chapter on worship for helpful information on questions six and seven.

8. This is probably true: Our guilt on this issue seems out of proportion with the biblical emphasis.

9. Yes. Sex was meant to unite two lives and get us into the heart and mind of another. Masturbation and the guilt we feel afterward increase the focus on ourselves. Furthermore, masturbation seems to lead to lust, even though it is possible to masturbate without lusting. Read the article on masturbation for more on this topic.

10. The point is not to take one option over another but to get people talking about a plan to stop — whatever plan they choose. It is also a chance for the group to discuss what they have done to try to stop.

11. Sometimes they are the same, but women's fantasies often have a more relational dimension added to the sexual.

12. The idea is that men struggle with lust, but women struggle with the power they have to make men lust. Discuss how a lack of modesty among women can be a stumbling block.

13. Discuss. Sexual purity as a lifestyle is clearly attainable, even if there are occasional mishaps. In fact, such a lifestyle seems attainable only when it, and nothing less, is the goal.

14. Discuss as a group.

15. You can be trusting in your own resolve or willpower to bring it about. You can also set yourself up for great guilt if you fail.

16. A godly commitment would be to fight, persevere and never give in to lust. Though the battle may take a while, we can commit to never making a truce with lust. See the article called "My Mind's Made Up" for more on this.

17. Share what you have written and ask others to share their commitments.

**Week 3: Temptation**

As preparation, read the article "When Tempted."

1. He wants the reader to recognize his own responsibility as it relates to sin. The truth is, once we are hooked on a sin such as sex, Satan doesn't need to be involved. We do a fine job ourselves.

2. This is just for discussion. Satan is probably more involved at crucial junctures, like when we are just beginning to pursue purity.

3. You might look at the story of Nehemiah. As Nehemiah attempts to rebuild the wall, he is attacked at the beginning of the venture, the middle, and the end. These are the most strategic times of any project. Other strategic times are when we are physically or emotionally weak or vulnerable.

4. This is just for discussion. For the discerning, a greater degree of attraction, "coincidence" or oppressiveness may be felt.

5. Physical attraction is normal, healthy and from God. Evil desires are plans to take for ourselves that which God has not given, or plans to act out and satisfy our lust. Lust is "over passion," going beyond simple attraction to the point of fantasizing.

6. You might share some examples to encourage the group to be vulnerable.

7. You'd blame God for your failure and be angry at him for having placed you in the tempting situation.

8. We never have to sin, but the clear implication of this verse is that the way God makes this possible is by keeping us out of certain temptations where we don't have the resources or capacity to say, "No."

9. Discuss examples from your own lives.

10. Some of the great lies or rationalizations about sexual sin relate to thinking the opposite: that we are unique; that we have special problems; or that our temptations are more difficult.

11. Adam and Eve were tempted to distrust that God had their best interest in mind. They were tempted to believe God was withholding something good from them and that God didn't trust them with knowledge.

12. Some examples of lies we believe could be that God doesn't care that he didn't provide for you, that he won't discipline you, or that he is testing or tempting you.

13. Conception seems to refer to the construction of a plan, or the intentionality to follow through on the sin.

14. Discuss. Many sexual temptations are like this.

15. Look for people to have some kind of action point for this question.

Close the study by asking if there are specific temptations the group could pray about together.

### Week 4: Sex

1. Paul's primary purpose in writing was to say that, while they were not sinning, there was still room for growth.

2. Sanctified means to be made holy. Sexual immorality is a general term referring to anything that deviates from God's design for sex. Passionate lust is a lust that has been cultivated and has now become a very large sexual appetite. It also speaks of unbridled desire. Heathen are the nonreligious, the godless.

3. Specific challenges might include the Internet, pornographic movies and lyrics, as well as the very late age we tend to marry in

our culture. There is no right answer for the next two questions.

4. Have the group look up the verses and summarize.

5. A key thought is that our bodies are the temples of the Holy Spirit. Therefore, we have a responsibility to keep our bodies pure from sexual immorality. Our bodies belong to God.

6. Someday the brother or sister with whom you've been intimate may get married and belong to another. Sexual immorality from this perspective is like robbery: taking something that doesn't belong to you.

7. Discuss. It might be nothing more than a kiss.

8. This is just for discussion. There are pros and cons to engaging an ex-girlfriend on this issue. It might be best left alone.

9. Discuss.

10. The phrase contains a warning and an exhortation to be holy. This imperative to be holy, coupled with Paul's reminder that God gives us his Holy Spirit, seems to be a reminder that we are to remember that the Holy Spirit indwells our bodies, making sexual impurity, hopefully, unthinkable.

11. It is how God designed sex and therefore how it works best. It is a degree of intimacy best protected by the commitments of marriage. It also reflects our relationship with God, which is purity and intimacy reserved for God alone. Reading the article "An Original Design" may be helpful for this question.

12. Give people the freedom to discuss this. Basically, anything that begins to cause sexual arousal is stepping over the line of lust. Read the article "Just How Far" for more insight on this issue.

13. This is for discussion, but you want to see that people have

used the Scriptures to inform their standard.

14. This issue is discussed in "Just How Far," so you should probably read it over before the study. You might want to copy the article and give it out to the group to take home and read.

### Week 5: Grow

1. It is called sanctification.

2. This is really a gauge to see what people think is the most critical element of our spiritual growth.

3. Discuss.

4. One extreme in relying on God's part is expecting a miracle — waiting for God to heal or change us. The other extreme is simply trying to live a disciplined life, assuming all responsibility for our holiness.

5. You should be hearing things from the group concerning God's motivating, leading, empowering, encouraging and convicting.

6. Yes. Read the article "The Way We Grow." Praise, worship, thanksgiving, time in the Word, the yielding of our hearts and our ability to be taught, among other things, all increase the Spirit's influence in our life and our sensitivity to him.

7. Philippians 2:1 speaks of disunity breaking the bond of the Spirit. Sin in general hinders the Spirit's influence.

8. Busyness, media or worry would be some examples of things that can distract our hearts and minds so we cannot hear the Spirit's leading.

9. A person's character is really the sum total of his habits. You and I become the type of person who does or thinks or feels a

certain way given certain circumstances. As our habits change, so too does our character.

10. Discuss as a group.

11. We learn about God through the process of becoming holy. We grow in faith. We understand how to rely on God. We understand the depth and dynamics of sin in our lives. We grow in understanding of God's grace as well as our thankfulness for it.

12. The passages discuss some of the reasons God didn't simply give the land to the Israelites: they would become self-reliant; they wouldn't be thankful; they would forget God; and they wouldn't fully own the land they had not helped clear.

13. Discuss as a group.

14. You're looking to see if people have begun to grow in their understanding of the balance between God's part and our part and the many nuances of the partnership. Make sure to read the article "The Way We Grow."

15. We must never cease in the battle for our holiness and never tolerate areas of sin in our life. It is okay to fail, but it is not okay not to fight or to passively allow sin to control our lives.

16. Here is one reference of hope: "Dear friends, now we are children of God, and what we will be has not yet been made known. But we know that when he appears, we shall be like him, for we shall see him as he is" (1 John 3:2). You can find others.

### Week 6: Help

In preparation for the study, read over the article "Blood Brothers."

1. It's hard to know the answer to this, but regardless, isolation

opens a door for spiritual attack on our lives.

2. When we are isolated, we are shut off from relationships of accountability. When isolated, our reasoning is much easier to impair. There is spiritual power and protection within the Christian community.

3. Relationships take effort, and people can become annoying, amongst other things. To get the group talking, share your own reasons for why you isolate yourself.

4. Our spiritual lives can become very self-centered and self-absorbed apart from others.

5. Discuss as a group. People can begin to doubt their salvation.

6. Media makes us momentarily less conscious of our isolation and boredom, but ultimately it increases both.

7. This is just for discussion.

8. Christian community is a place where we are encouraged to walk with God and where we are known by others. It is also a place where we get and give encouragement and learn about God.

9. This is just an exercise. People might end up saying all kinds of ridiculous things, which is quite all right. The point is still served that there is enjoyment and life in being known.

10. Confessing to others helps us to feel forgiven. It also can provide accountability and prayer, two things that are extremely helpful in attaining victory in the sexual area.
11. The focus of 1 John 1:9 is confessing to God and being cleansed. The focus of James 5:16 is confessing to others and getting better.

12. Even if you need to connect members of the group together, or suggest that the group pairs up or meets in smaller groups of

three persons, make sure everyone has somebody with whom they can share their sin and struggles.

13. All of us will have to give an account someday before God. Relationships of accountability are ones we've chosen in which to disclose our lives in total honesty. These relationships provide strength, prayer, help and encouragement and ultimately enable us to give a good account before God.

14. E-mail or I.M. one another at night to keep each other accountable while on the computer. Meet regularly to discuss sexual struggles. Decide together on certain practices and standards to guard purity.

15. Grace is expressing unconditional forgiveness. Truth means we ask difficult questions like "What will you do differently so that this doesn't happen again?" Truth is upholding standards, while grace grants forgiveness if they are broken.

16. People will tend more to one side or the other.

17. Have the group share what they've listed.

Application: Have the group sign up for Covenant Eyes at www. covenanteyes.com. This is a Christian ministry, with software that automatically forwards a log of the websites you've visited to two friends. Ask the individuals in your group to select two friends to be their accountability partners.

## Week 7: Truth

1. Have people share their answers with the group.

2. Truth's meaning is either the truth about God, truth in general, the truth of the gospel or the truth of Scripture. The point you are making is that the truth of Scripture is not the only way the Bible speaks of truth.

3. Discuss as a group.

4. Discuss as a group.

5. Truth can make us feel free, probably because we feel trapped by sins and lies. These lies keep us from being known. Lies separate us from God and others and even separate us internally.

6. You might want to look in the account of the temptation of Jesus in Scripture. Satan seems to tempt him by declaring his identity and glory, without the suffering of the cross. This is exactly what Peter is proposing in these verses in the book of Mark. If Satan tempted Jesus in this way, it must be a very real temptation for him.

7. Jesus states the truth of the temptation. He labels it for what it is and uncovers Satan's scheme. Though he fights with truth, it is not a passage of Scripture.

8. You want people to think of who they might tell or bring into their struggles. It could also be that they do what Jesus did when tempted. Another component would be complete honesty with yourself. When your mind is beginning to rationalize your behavior, then label what you are doing. Read over the article "A Belt of Truth."

9. This should be a powerful exercise and worth scrapping other questions to make time for. You want to give people the opportunity to share with the group what they have written, as well as the

option not to share.

10. The truth of Scripture has the power to renew the mind and stimulate the heart and motivate the will toward loving God. It also brings conviction of sin and repentance.

11. Give the group a chance to find some. Look up a few in advance of the study that you could share. Include promises of eternal life, the idea that God's ways are life-giving to our souls, etc.

12. Discuss.

13. You aren't looking for a correct answer. It might be a new idea for some that may be of benefit.

14. Scripture's efficacy might be enhanced by meditating on the truth of what it is saying, choosing to act in faith on what it says and growing in our maturity in Christ. (Over time, we grow in our knowledge and trust of God and the truth of Scripture.)

15. Have people share their points of application.

## ADDITIONAL RESOURCES

**Internet Use**

**Filtering** Filtering proactively detects and blocks objectionable content. (Examples: If your child does an Internet search for "naked girls," it will block the search; If your child mistakenly clicks a link to a pornographic web site, it will block access to the site.)

**Accountability** Accountability software tracks web sites visited from different devices and then prepares and delivers regular reports. (Example: If your child visits a pornographic web site or performs a search for "naked girls," the accountability software will note it and include it in a report emailed to you.)

**OpenDNS** (www.opendns.com) uses filtering to automatically block objectionable web sites for every device connected to your home network. It is activated by making a small change to the settings on your existing router. OpenDNS Home VIP is the optional, premier solution and costs $19.95 per year.

**Books**

*Surfing for God* by Michael Cusick
*Every Man's Battle* by Steve Aterburn
*The War Within* by Robert Daniels
*Pure Desire* by Ted Roberts
*Finally Free: Fighting for Purity with the Power of Grace* by Heath Lambert

**Websites**
FightTheNewDrug.org
Fight the New Drug is a group of passionate and innovative problem-solvers who want to make a difference in the world. Their mission is to raise awareness on the harmful effects of pornography through creative mediums.

CovenantEyes.com
Covenant Eyes tracks the web sites visited by your computers and mobile devices and sends regular email reports; it also offers optional filtering that can be configured specifically for each member of your family.

BrushfireFoundation.org
A non-profit ministry helping those impacted by sexual brokenness to discover, reclaim and live out their created identity in Christ.

**Articles**
*The New Narcotic* by Morgan Bennett
www.thepublicdiscourse.com

*The Gospel and Sex* by Tim Keller
www.gospelinlife.com

*The Porn-Free Family Plan* by Tim Challies
www.challies.com

## "PORN'S EFFECT ON THE BRAIN"
### BY AUSTIN ROSS

———————

Porn is the 4th-most common reason people give for going on the Internet.

It makes up 25% of all search engine requests.

And it's changing your brain.

In a lot of ways, porn acts similarly to a drug. There's this thing called dopamine, which is a hormone and neurotransmitter — and dopamine gets released into our brains when we do things that either sustain life (like eating) or things that create life (like sex). The dopamine that's released becomes correlated to specific acts. The more dopamine that's released, the stronger the urge to keep doing the thing that released the dopamine in the first place. After extreme levels of dopamine get released, this protein called Delta FosB starts to build up, which leads to a more intense cycle of binging and craving.

It ends up creating a feedback loop, a sort-of merry-go-round that spins faster and faster over time.

Don't get me wrong — dopamine is actually a good thing. It's a God-given reward system that helps regulate our activity, and points us towards things that are genuinely good and joy-giving.

But for those of us alive in the 21st century (which I hope includes all of you), the amount of dopamine we have access to is historically unheard of.

Part of that is because of the nature of Internet porn. Researchers are only just realizing that pornography addiction is a thing — but porn has been around in various forms for probably as long as humans have existed...so how is it we're just now seeing significant negative effects?

The answer is in the Internet's ability to constantly surprise us.

You see this all over the place: we check our Twitter feed throughout the day to see what people are saying, websites like BuzzFeed post an incessant stream of articles and quizzes, and we find ourselves on Amazon, practically salivating over whatever new thing we don't have but definitely need.

Internet porn functions in exactly the same way; it's a labyrinth of constant novelty. You can click and click and click, and never watch the same video twice. The constant sense of novelty, that feeling of watching something new, essentially means we can spend hours and hours watching porn while a constant stream of dopamine gets released into our brains.

And it's all so easy to access.

That's a little disheartening.

But there is good news — just like your brain is changed by porn, it can change back. The less you watch, the less you want to watch. The dopamine your brain releases will start to get redirected in other, healthier ways. Studies are indicating that you'll feel better about yourself, your relationships with others will be healthier, and you'll have more time to be productive.

So what are you waiting for? Ask Jesus to continue to change you, and invite a few close friends to walk with you through this struggle. Your brain will thank you.

## "THE GOSPEL OF SEX"
### BY TIM KELLER

---

Today's young adults take for granted that normal people will have sex if they are in a romantic relationship. Even those who speak of themselves as "conservative" or "traditional" simply mean they will not sleep with a boyfriend or girlfriend until later in the relationship. The Christian ethic of abstinence outside of marriage is considered at best laughably unrealistic, and at worst pathological and abnormal. Christians who profess the biblical sex ethic can expect to be met with incredulity, sarcasm, or hostility. Basically, the mainstream view is that adultery is wrong because it hurts a spouse but that there's nothing wrong with sex between two loving, consenting unmarried adults. And as Christian leaders, we are finding this view to be widespread inside the Christian community as well. How do we respond?

**The Pervasive Understanding of the Bible**
It is rather typical to hear Christians say, "I know that the Ten

Commandments forbid adultery, but the Bible doesn't really forbid sex between two unmarried people." The idea of premarital sex was l outrageous in ancient cultures, however, that it was simply assumed in many passages. For example, in 1 Corinthians 7, Paul wished more Christians would choose, as he has, a single life. He believed there were great advantages for singles in the work of the kingdom. "I would like you to be free from concern. An unmarried man is concerned about the Lord's affairs — how he can please the Lord. But a married man is "concerned about . . . how he can please his wife" (1 Cor. 7:32–33). He wished more people were like him (1 Cor. 7:7, 26, 32) and stated, "It is good for them to stay unmarried, as I am. But if they cannot control themselves, they should marry, for it is better to marry than to burn with passion" (1 Cor. 7:8–9).

In other words, Paul simply assumed that a single person would be celibate. If you cannot stay celibate, he said, you should get married. There is not even a hint that a single person should be having sex. The idea that Jesus Christ, as a first century Jew, could have thought that sex between unmarried people was permissible is historically laughable.

## THE MEANING OF *PORNEIA*

Still, we can be sympathetic to Christians who find it hard to cite chapter and verse against premarital sex. One of the problems involves the difficulty of translating the word *porneia* or *pornos* In the older King James Version this word was usually translated "fornication," but that word is archaic. Modern translations have rendered the word as "sexual immorality." But that is too vague a term, as can be seen from 1 Corinthians 6:9 ("Neither fornicators nor idolaters nor adulterers . . . will inherit the kingdom of God") and Hebrews 13:4 ("Marriage should be honored . . . for God will judge the adulterer and all fornicators").

We see in these and many other such references that fornication means something more than just adultery. The authors are clearly thinking of different kinds of sins, or they wouldn't be distinguishing between these groups of persons in the lists. Nearly all commentators tell us that *pornoi* has reference to those who engage in sexual relationships outside of marriage. The word *moichoi* "denotes those who are unfaithful to the vows of commitment expressed in marriage." So *porneia* refers to any sex other than sex with your own spouse. In other words, while adultery is always fornication, fornication includes premarital sex as well as extramarital sex or adultery.

The biblical condemnation of "fornication" or sex outside of marriage is comprehensive. Paul's epistles contain so many reminders to Christians to abstain from premarital sex that it is obvious his readers lived in a culture similar to our own.

## THE UNITY IN THE UNITIES

One of the ways some Christians try to mute the impact of biblical teaching is to point out that *porneia* is also translated (in some contexts) "harlotry" or "prostitution." Therefore, it is occasionally maintained that "fornication" only means sex with prostitutes, not sex between two people who love one another. But Paul's case study of sex with a prostitute in 1 Corinthians 6 is very instructive and disproves this reasoning: "Do you not know that he who unites himself with a prostitute is one with her in body? For it is said, 'The two will become one flesh' " (1 Cor. 6:17).

Clearly "one flesh" must mean something different here from mere physical insertion, or Paul would be reciting a mere tautology: "Don't you know that when you have physical union with a prostitute you are having physical union with a prostitute?" So what does it mean? "'One flesh' . . . refers to the personal union of man with woman, woman with man, at all levels of their lives." To become "one flesh" means to become one new person — a new human unit. So when Paul used the word pornos about the case of sex with a prostitute, he cannot mean that one is automatically married in some kind of magical way. Rather, Paul is decrying the monstrosity of physical oneness without all the other kinds of oneness that every sex act should mirror. "Paul... here

**207**

displays a psychological insight into human sexuality, which is altogether exceptional by first century standards... he insists that it is an act which... engages and expresses the whole personality in such a way as to constitute an unique mode of self-disclosure and self commitment."

In short, sex with a prostitute is wrong because every sex act is supposed to reflect an absolute and complete covenant unity. There must be no physical union unless there is also every other kind — a legal, economic, personal, emotional, and spiritual union. There must not be one unity without all the rest. Likewise, C.S. Lewis likened sex without marriage to tasting without swallowing and digesting.